KT-502-630

# THE BIG ready steady COOK BOOK

BBC BOOKS

This book is published to accompany the television series Ready Steady Cook
which is produced by Bazal Productions Ltd for the BBC
Executive Producer: Linda Clifford
Producer: Mary Ramsay

Published by BBC Books, an imprint of BBC Worldwide Ltd,
Woodlands, 80 Wood Lane, London W12 0TT

First published in 1997
Compiled by Bazal Productions
Reprinted 1997
Reprinted 1998

Recipes copyright © 1997
Patrick Anthony • Ross Burden • Richard Cawley
Mark Gregory • Ainsley Harriott • Valentina Harris • Alastair Little
James Martin • Nick Nairn • Thane Prince • Paul Rankin • Anthony Tobin
Brian Turner • Phil Vickery • Lesley Waters • Kevin Woodford
Antony Worrall Thompson

The moral right of the authors has been asserted.

Photographs by Juliet Piddington,
copyright © 1997 BBC Worldwide Ltd
Foreword copyright © 1997 Fern Britton
Photograph on page 103, copyright © *The Telegraph* Colour Library

All rights reserved. No part of this book may be reproduced in any form or by
any means, without permission in writing from the publisher, except by a
reviewer who may quote brief passages in a review.

ISBN 0 563 38380 1

General Editor: Silvana Franco
Home Economist: Sarah Ramsbottom, assisted by Francesca Onnis
Stylist: Marian Price

Printed and bound in Great Britain by Butler & Tanner Ltd, Frome and London
Colour separations by Radstock Reproductions Ltd, Midsomer Norton
Jacket and printed paper case printed by Lawrence Allen Ltd,
Weston-super-Mare

Recipe illustrated on page 2:
Alastair Little's *Granddad's Criss-cross Pork* (see page 152)
Recipe illustrated on back cover:
Nick Nairn's *Swanky Salmon* (see page 53)

Over 100 of the recipes in this book have never been published before. The 32 recipes on the
following pages have previously appeared in Ready Steady Cook books 1, 2, 3 or 4:
pages 16, 21, 28, 29, 37, 38, 40, 44, 54, 60, 66, 76, 80, 85, 93, 97, 100, 108, 112, 113,
115, 117, 120, 121, 132, 144, 156, 160, 168, 173, 180, 190.

# Contents

Foreword      6

Who's Who on Ready Steady Cook      7

The Ready Steady Cook Larder      9

Vegetarian Dishes      10

Fish and Shellfish      46

Poultry and Game      82

Meat Dishes      118

Desserts      158

Index      191

# Foreword

Welcome to **The Big Ready Steady Cook Book**. Every page is bursting with flavour, colour and inspiration for even the most unconfident of cooks – believe me I write from personal experience.

It's three years since we started **Ready Steady Cook** on television. A handful of top chefs agreed to put their reputations on the line by making something delicious from five pounds' worth of mysterious and often eclectic ingredients, in only twenty minutes. Boy did they rise to the challenge! I can't think of a single chef who has failed to finish in all the five hundred programmes we have made (although I have tasted a few raw potatoes and some crispy pasta in that time). On top of that they patiently answer my constant questions.

Over the last three years you and I have grown to love all our chefs. The glorious Ainsley 'what's he like?' Harriott; Antony 'the arsonist' Worrall Thompson; Brian 'I hate puds' Turner; Kevin 'globe trotting' Woodford; Patrick 'Inspector Gadget' Anthony; Richard Cawley for his terrible jokes; Lesley Waters for her victory wiggles … Not to mention the heart throbs Anthony Tobin, Paul Rankin, Nick Nairn, Phil Vickery and James Martin … I could go on. Each one has their own style and a bottomless pit of knowledge and tips.

In this bumper book they'll guide you through the extra professional touches that they don't have time to explain on the programme and tell you about some of their own favourites. Ross Burden's five favourite flavours of the East, Lesley Waters' five favourite sandwiches and Paul Rankin's five favourite presentation tips.

Whether you're a student on a budget, a harried parent cooking for a hungry family or simply cooking for one, I hope this book fills your heart with confidence and inspiration and your tums with delicious grub. Go on, you can do it. Are you Ready? Steady? Cook!

## Fern Britton

*Presenter,* **Ready Steady Cook**

*P.S. Before you ask. No, I promise you, not one of them knows what's in the bag before it's tipped out in front of them!*

# Who's Who on Ready Steady Cook

## PATRICK ANTHONY

Probably best known for his many news-reporting appearances on Anglia Television and for his own cookery series *Patrick's Pantry*, Patrick has now earned himself a very loyal following among the **Ready Steady Cook** viewers eager to learn about his latest gadgetry discovery.

## ROSS BURDEN

New Zealand-born Ross has many accolades to his name, including being credited by *Company Magazine* as one of the UK's most eligible bachelors! A very cosmopolitan and well-travelled chef, Ross is self-taught and first began his television career when he reached the final of BBC's *Masterchef* programme.

## RICHARD CAWLEY

Richard's artistic temperament is evident in both his cookery and his flamboyant dress. He trained at art school and was happy to turn his creativity to food. Richard thoroughly enjoys **Ready Steady Cook,** particularly his banter with Fern, and is usually found competing alongside his regular opponent Patrick Anthony.

## MARK GREGORY

Landing the title of British Chef of the Year in 1988, Mark Gregory has gone on to enjoy an exciting career encompassing television appearances, publishing his own books and an active involvement in many top restaurants. He is currently Head Chef at T'SU, a contemporary Japanese restaurant in London.

## AINSLEY HARRIOTT

Ainsley is one of television's all-time most popular personalities, scooping award after award for his amiable style and natural cookery instinct. The fact that Ainsley has also worked as a stand-up comedian is evident in his humorous approach to cookery and the instant rapport he develops with every **Ready Steady Cook** contestant.

## VALENTINA HARRIS

The UK's authority on Italian regional food, Valentina is also the author of several top-selling books. She is an accomplished cookery demonstrator and teacher and appears on many television and radio programmes.

## ALASTAIR LITTLE

One of Britain's leading chefs and author of the award-winning book *Keep It Simple*, Alastair Little is one of **Ready Steady Cook's** popular occasional presenters. The essence of his style is that of the classical Mediterranean kitchen, although Alastair always injects a contemporary twist with key '90s ingredients.

## JAMES MARTIN

**Ready Steady Cook's** latest and youngest recruit, James is already proving to be a big hit with the programme's student viewers. Although aged just 24, James has already notched up appearances on *Food and Drink* and many other television programmes.

## NICK NAIRN

Scotland's youngest Michelin-starred chef Nick Nairn has a fast, furious pace that keeps the **Ready Steady Cook** contestants on their toes, and with his famed fetish for setting his food on fire, he offers a great deal of entertainment as well as winning recipes.

## THANE PRINCE

Thane's career as one of the country's top food writers has led her to all corners of the globe where she has developed a unique style encompassing an eclectic blend of cuisines. Alongside her regular **Ready Steady Cook** and other television appearances she writes for many newspapers and magazines.

## PAUL RANKIN

Along with his wife Jeanne, inspiring chef Paul Rankin has been awarded Northern Ireland's first ever Michelin Star and their restaurant Roscoff has landed the Courvoisier Restaurant of the Year award. He has travelled across the globe gaining insights into Japanese and Asian food that are evident in his **Ready Steady Cook** recipes.

## ANTHONY TOBIN

Training under Nico Ladenis for several years, Anthony Tobin has learned to cook classical French food under one of the world's most famous classical French chefs. Currently appearing on **Ready Steady Cook,** Anthony is also Head Chef at the Dining Room in Reigate, Surrey, as well as working on his first book.

## BRIAN TURNER

One of **Ready Steady Cook**'s original team, Brian is still very much a 'hands-on' chef at his own restaurant Turner's in London's Knightsbridge. He developed his classical style of cookery in many of the world's top-ranking kitchens including Simpsons in the Strand and the Beau Rivage Palace in Switzerland.

## PHIL VICKERY

Head Chef and Director of the acclaimed Castle Hotel, Phil Vickery is carving out a name for himself as one of Britain's most talented chefs and television personalities. He has just won the Egon Ronay Chef of the Year Award 1998.

## LESLEY WATERS

Her bubbly nature and lively personality make Lesley Waters one of television's most popular female chefs. Her varied career includes working as head teacher at Leith's School of Food and Wine in London, writing several books including BBC titles such as *Fifteen Minute Feasts*, and working part-time as an aerobics teacher.

## KEVIN WOODFORD

Another member of the original **Ready Steady Cook** team and a regular face on television, Kevin is the star of several programmes including BBC's *Can't Cook, Won't Cook*. Kevin is also co-owner of the prestigious Woodford's restaurant overlooking Douglas Bay on the Isle of Man.

## ANTONY WORRALL THOMPSON

Antony's colourful career as cookery expert not only embraces his television work but has also incorporated being head chef and proprietor of many award-winning restaurants. His ever-evolving projects currently include being a regular judge for the Académie Culinaire's Annual Award of Excellence. He also organises the Young Chef of the Year competition and offers sought-after apprenticeships to budding new talents.

### Healthy Eating

If you are trying to cut calories or reduce the fat in your diet, it doesn't mean you have to miss out on taste or cooking these recipes. Check out some healthy alternatives. Buy trimmed or extra-lean meat and bacon, and remove the skin from chicken pieces. Use half-fat hard cheeses and semi-skimmed milk.For everyday use, why not try low-fat fromage frais and low-fat natural yoghurt as substitutes for cream and crème fraîche. Opt for low-fat soft cheese instead of cream cheese. Cook with sunflower, vegetable or olive oil in place of butter where possible.

# The Ready Steady Cook Larder

 If you keep your larder stocked with all these ingredients you will only need to buy the items shown next to this symbol in the recipes.

**Arrowroot:** good for thickening clear sauces, it should be dissolved in a little water before use.

**Baking powder**

**Balsamic vinegar:** this sweet-flavoured, Italian aged vinegar proves a popular choice for salad dressings.

**Bay leaves:** an invaluable addition to stocks and sauces.

**Beef stock cubes**

**Bicarbonate of soda**

**Bottle of red wine:** great for gravies and sauces.

**Bottle of white wine**

**Bread, fresh white:** make into crumbs for stuffing, bake for croûtons or bruschetta or turn it into a summer pudding – the RSC chefs' growing uses for a humble loaf of bread go on and on.

**Brown sugar**

**Butter:** always choose unsalted butter when making those glossy, reduced sauces that chefs love, or the finished result will be too salty.

**Cardamom pods**

**Caster sugar**

**Cayenne pepper:** adds colour and a little heat wherever it's dusted.

**Chicken stock cubes**

**Chilli powder**

**Cocoa powder**

**Cornflour:** great thickening agent that doesn't have the starchy flavour of plain flour.

**Demerara sugar**

**Dijon mustard:** its mild flavour lends itself to marinades, dressings and sauces – a real store cupboard essential.

**Double cream:** more stable than single cream, this is far less likely to curdle under the heat of the studio lights and, of course, can be whipped up in a few seconds to help make perfect puddings.

**Dried mixed herbs**

**Dried oregano:** Italians believe that dried oregano is superior to its fresh counterpart and it's certainly true that a pinch of this livens up any tomato sauce no end.

**Eggs, medium**

**English mustard**

**Garam masala:** this special blend of ground Indian spices has a very mild flavour that makes it useful for countless Asian dishes.

**Garlic:** fresh garlic is used in just about every savoury recipe ever created by our chefs.

**Golden syrup:** perfect for puds, pancakes and Nick Nairn's savoury sauces.

**Granulated sugar:** the first choice for brûlées and caramel-crack toppings.

**Greek yoghurt:** the mild flavour and creamy texture of Greek yoghurt makes it a very valuable ingredient – it has a higher fat content than other yoghurts so is also less likely to curdle during cooking.

**Herbs:** chopped and stirred into just about every savoury dish, a simple sprig of fresh herbs is one of the all-time classic garnishes; includes basil, chervil, coriander, dill, parsley, rosemary, sage and thyme.

**Honey:** great for sweet glazes and sauces.

**Icing sugar**

**Lamb stock cubes**

**Lemons and limes:** the juice and grated rind is used frequently to add zing to all manner of dishes.

**Milk**

**Olive oil:** this Mediterranean staple is the chefs' number one choice when it comes to dressings and light frying. Save extra virgin olive oils for dressings only.

**Oranges:** squeeze out their juice, toss them in caramel or slice into a salad – they're pretty useful to have around.

**Peppercorns**

**Plain flour:** for dusting and batters.

**Red wine vinegar:** sauces and salad dressings.

**Selection of dried spices:** including cinnamon, cloves, ginger and nutmeg.

**Self-raising flour:** get those baking hats on!

**Sesame oil:** used to add a touch of nutty oriental flavour to stir-fries.

**Soy sauce:** another oriental essential, perfect for marinades, dressings, dips and stir-fries.

**Sunflower oil:** for all manner of frying.

**Tabasco sauce:** in its original red-hot format and the milder green Jalapeño variety – a dash of this adds a kick to any dish.

**Tomato purée**

**Tomato ketchup:** an invaluable sauce of colour and sweetness.

**Turmeric:** mild-flavoured spice with a bold yellow colour – great added to water before cooking rice or potatoes.

**Vanilla pods**

**Vegetable oil**

**Vegetable stock cubes:** the simplest base for soups, stews and sauces.

**Wholegrain mustard:** texture and flavour for marinades, dressings and sauces.

**Worcestershire sauce**

# VEGETARIAN DISHES

# Down Mexico Way

Flour tortillas, onion, tinned cherry tomatoes, tinned refried beans, avocado, pickled Jalapeño chillies.

Tortillas are so often a clumsy dish – this recipe for stacked tortillas is a sophisticated way to serve them, with a good guacamole and refried beans.

**SERVES 2**

12 flour tortillas
3 tablespoons olive oil
1 onion, finely chopped
2 garlic cloves, finely chopped
400 g tin of cherry tomatoes
225 g tin of refried beans
1 avocado, stoned and halved
1 tablespoon Greek yoghurt
4 tablespoons double cream
Juice of ½ lime
1 tablespoon chopped fresh dill
2 tablespoons white wine
290 g jar pickled Jalapeño chillies
Salt and freshly ground black pepper

Using a 7.5 cm (3 in) pastry cutter, stamp three circles out of each tortilla. Warm the tortilla discs in a very hot griddle pan for a few seconds on each side until lightly browned; set aside to cool.

To make the tomato sauce, heat 1 tablespoon of the olive oil in a frying-pan and cook the onion and garlic for 3–4 minutes until softened. Pour in the tomatoes, bring to the boil and simmer for 5 minutes until thickened and pulpy. Season to taste.

Place the refried beans in a small pan and heat through gently. Stir in about a quarter of the tomato sauce and cook gently for a further 5 minutes.

To make the avocado purée, scoop the avocado flesh out of the shells and place half the flesh in a food processor with the yoghurt, cream and lime juice. Blend until smooth, then stir in the dill and salt and pepper to taste.

To make the avocado dressing, mash half of the remaining avocado with the white wine and remaining 2 tablespoons of olive oil; season to taste. Cut the remaining avocado into small dice.

Stack the tortilla discs with a layer of beans, the tomato sauce, the avocado purée and the diced avocado. Spoon round the avocado dressing, garnish with the chopped Jalapeño chillies and serve.

Avocado is rich in vitamins and very versatile – add chillies or toss with tomatoes to make great dips and salsas.

**ANTHONY TOBIN**

# Saucy Soufflé Tartlets

To present this dish of soufflé goats' cheese tartlets with crispy leeks and red pepper and walnut sauce at its best, it must be served as soon as it is cooked. If you're planning to serve it as a dinner-party starter, make the tartlet cases and red pepper dressing ahead of time, then simply cook the soufflés and crispy leeks once your guests are seated. *Illustrated on page 10.*

 Ready-made shortcrust pastry, leeks, red pepper, walnuts, soft goats' cheese.

Roll the pastry out on a floured surface to a thickness of 5 mm (¼ in) and use to line four 7.5 cm (3 in) pastry cases. Bake blind for 12–15 minutes until crisp and golden.

Meanwhile, separate the sliced leeks into rings and place in a bowl with the milk; set aside.

To make the soufflés, place the milk and cheese in a small pan and heat gently, without boiling, until the cheese melts. Stir in the slaked cornflour, cayenne and plenty of salt and pepper. Slowly bring to the boil, stirring until thickened. Pour the mixture into a large bowl and beat in the egg yolks and chives. In a separate bowl, whisk the egg whites until they form soft peaks and carefully fold into the cheese mixture. Pour into four well-buttered 7.5 cm (3 in) ramekins and bake for 6–8 minutes until golden and risen.

Meanwhile, heat the olive oil in large frying-pan and cook the pepper strips over a high heat for 4–5 minutes until beginning to blacken. Add the walnuts and cook for 1–2 minutes until golden, then stir in the sugar and balsamic vinegar. Season to taste and keep warm.

Drain the leeks and toss with the seasoned flour to coat. Deep-fry in hot sunflower oil for 2–3 minutes until crisp and golden. Drain on kitchen paper.

To serve, place a tartlet case in the centre of each of four plates, arrange the crispy leeks around the edge and spoon over the warm dressing. Turn out the soufflés and place one in each pastry case. Garnish with the chives and serve immediately.

 Choose any soft cheese labelled 'chèvre' for this recipe. It is guaranteed to be made from pure goats' milk and will have that distinctive, tangy flavour that makes these soufflés so delicious.

**SERVES 4 AS A STARTER**

250 g (9 oz) ready-made shortcrust pastry
2 leeks, thinly sliced
6 tablespoons milk
2 tablespoons olive oil
1 red pepper, seeded and cut into thin strips
1 tablespoon chopped walnuts
1 tablespoon caster sugar
½ teaspoon balsamic vinegar
2 tablespoons seasoned plain flour
150 ml (5 fl oz) sunflower oil for deep-frying

**FOR THE SOUFFLÉS**
175 ml (6 fl oz) milk
100 g (4 oz) soft goats' cheese
2 teaspoons cornflour dissolved in a little water
½ teaspoon cayenne
3 eggs, separated
1 tablespoon snipped fresh chives
Salt and freshly ground black pepper

# Tips for the Best-dressed Tables

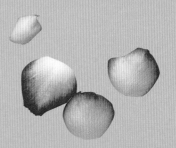

**N**othing is more glamorous than an all-white table, so if you are buying china and glass for the first time, don't be tempted to buy something decorative and fashionable – you will tire of it as quickly as out-of-date clothing. Choose the simplest all-white china you can find, the plainest of glasses and classic cutlery.

For everyday use, you will never get bored with classic simplicity and for special occasions, add the luxury of a freshly laundered white table cloth and napkins (not paper), some candles and a few very simple flowers. The effect will never be less than stunning. The same simple setting on plain wood, a coloured cloth or a vivid modern print (look for inexpensive remnants of unusual dress fabrics) will instantly add a fresh mood and totally different look for minimal cost.

Once you have your 'classic white collection' as the perfect basis for endless variations, it is fun to start a 'special collection' of plates or cups and saucers. These need not necessarily be antiques or even valuable, but odd, single pieces can be picked up for next to nothing in junk shops and boot fairs. If you choose a colour theme like blue and white you can mix all kinds of styles and

patterns together with great effect. Use against a white background, pick out the predominant colour in the china or choose a wild, contrasting colour for fabulous effect.

Candles always add an immense sense of glamour and occasion to any table setting. For a special dinner, light the whole room just with candles. If you buy them in bulk, it need not cost a fortune (IKEA candles are not only very cheap, but also non-drip). Either use just one colour (white always look luxurious if used lavishly) or use a wild selection of colours, shapes and sizes grouped together as a table centrepiece – try and get the heights as varied as possible, not just with the candles but with the holders.

When it comes to flowers, a simple, dramatic but unusual touch is often more effective than spending hours on elaborate arrangements. Simply scatter flower petals (roses are ideal) all over a plain table cloth for a fabulous effect. Or try fallen leaves in all their rich colours for a splendid autumn setting. An extravagant mass of one kind of flower (whatever is cheap and in season) will add a spectacular touch, whilst a small,

tasteful selection of mixed blooms in the centre of the table will look very stylish. For a more personal touch, impress guests by arranging a miniature posy (wild flowers would be lovely) by each table setting (egg cups or sherry glasses make ideal miniature vases). Tie each with a small ribbon and invite your friends to take them home as a keepsake of a perfect evening.

Except for barbecues and picnics, fabric napkins are always a much better choice than paper ones. Make your own from inexpensive fabric remnants and simply fray the edges to make a small border of fringe if you are no good at sewing. A fabric ribbon always makes a delightful napkin ring particularly if you tuck a single flower or a sprig of herbs (thyme, bay or rosemary won't wilt quickly) under the bow.

Use a couple of tins of fabric dye and your washing machine to transform tired or stained white cloth or linen table cloths. Choose strong pastels. My favourite is a linen damask cloth bought cheaply at a junk market and now dyed a magnificent shade of deep rose pink.

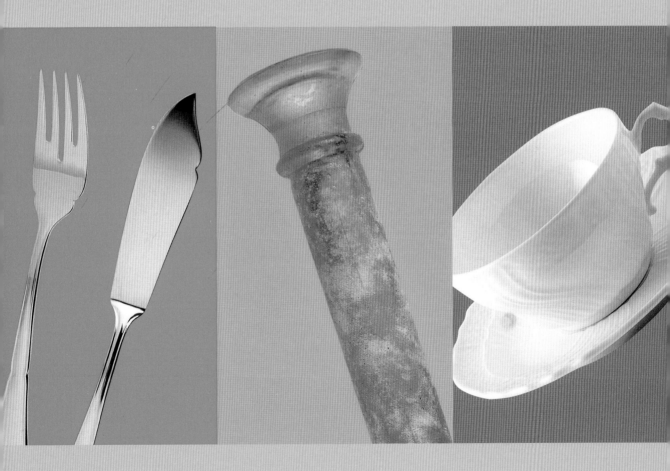

KEVIN WOODFORD

# Naughty Gnocchi with Spicy Tomato Sauce

Semolina, Parmesan, onion, red pepper, leek, tinned chopped tomatoes.

There are basically three types of gnocchi but this one is based around semolina and is for me the most interesting one to serve. You can use any cheese you like and try adding a handful of freshly snipped herbs to the raw gnocchi mixture.

### SERVES 2

450 ml (15 fl oz) milk
75 g (3 oz) semolina
1 egg yolk
25 g (1 oz) butter
1 tablespoon double cream
75 g (3 oz) Parmesan, grated
½ teaspoon freshly grated nutmeg

### FOR THE SAUCE

15 g (½ oz) butter
½ onion, finely chopped
½ red pepper, seeded and sliced
½ leek, sliced
1 garlic clove, crushed
1 tablespoon chopped fresh coriander
1 tablespoon chopped fresh parsley
400 g tin of chopped tomatoes
Few drops of Tabasco sauce
4 tablespoons tomato purée
Salt and freshly ground black pepper

To make the gnocchi, bring the milk to the boil and add the semolina, stirring continuously until the mixture thickens. Beat in the egg yolk, butter, cream and half of the Parmesan. Add nutmeg, salt and pepper to taste. Butter a small, shallow, heatproof dish, spoon in the semolina mixture and allow to cool.

To make the sauce, melt the butter in a pan and cook the onion, pepper, leek, garlic and herbs for 5 minutes until softened. Stir in the chopped tomatoes, Tabasco sauce and tomato purée, bring to the boil and simmer for 10 minutes, stirring occasionally. Add salt and pepper to taste.

Turn out the semolina mixture, then stamp out rounds using a 5 cm (2 in) pastry cutter. Return the circles to the same dish, arranging them in a single layer, and sprinkle over the remaining Parmesan. Place under a pre-heated grill for 4–5 minutes until the cheese is melted and golden brown.

To serve, transfer the gnocchi to a plate and spoon round the sauce.

Make almost-instant tomato sauces by gently heating together a carton of passata or creamed tomatoes with some fresh herbs or a crushed garlic clove, a drizzle of olive oil and plenty of black pepper.

## VALENTINA HARRIS
# Creamy Mushroom Risotto

A risotto is not designed to be light but is a rich and deliciously creamy dish. In Italy, where it is only ever served as a starter, it is usually followed by a very simple and extremely light second course. The traditional saying is 'il riso nasce nell'acqua e dev morir nel vino' (rice is born in water but must die in wine). In other words, always drink wine when eating risotto!

Dried porcini mushrooms, onion, risotto rice, fresh Parmesan, chestnut or open-cup mushrooms.

Stir the dried mushrooms into the boiling water, take off the heat and set aside to soak for 10 minutes. Drain, reserving the soaking liquid, and roughly chop the mushrooms.

Heat 2 tablespoons of the olive oil in a large pan and cook the herbs for 1 minute. Pour in the water and the reserved soaking liquid, then crumble in the stock cube and bring to the boil.

Meanwhile, melt the butter in a pan and cook the onion for 5 minutes until softened. Stir in the rice and cook for 1 minute. Add the soaked mushrooms and white wine, stirring until the liquid is absorbed. Keeping the heat fairly high, gradually add the hot stock a ladle at a time, stirring until the liquid is absorbed and the rice is tender and creamy – this process takes about 20 minutes. Stir in the Parmesan and cream and add salt and pepper to taste.

Heat the remaining olive oil in a large frying-pan and cook the mushrooms and garlic over a high heat for 2–3 minutes until golden brown. Stir in the chopped parsley and add salt and pepper to taste.

To serve, spoon the risotto into a large serving dish and scatter over the garlic mushrooms.

### SERVES 4

25 g (1 oz) dried porcini mushrooms
200 ml (7 fl oz) boiling water
4 tablespoons olive oil
3 fresh bay leaves
6 fresh sage leaves
3 fresh parsley sprigs
600 ml (1 pint) water
1 vegetable stock cube
25 g (1 oz) butter
1 onion, very finely chopped
450g (1 lb) risotto rice
150 ml (5 fl oz) white wine
100 g (4 oz) fresh Parmesan, grated
2 tablespoons double cream
250 g (9 oz) chestnut or open-cup mushrooms, sliced
2 garlic cloves, chopped
2 tablespoons chopped fresh parsley
Salt and freshly ground black pepper

There are several different types of risotto rice available including Arborio and Carnaroli. Good risotto rice is very starchy which is what gives the finished dish its lovely, creamy texture – the ideal grain has a floury exterior and nice, rounded appearance.

Creamy Mushroom Risotto (page 17)

**Hearty Cassoulet (page 20)**

# Hearty Cassoulet

Green or brown lentils, vegetable suet, Cheddar, onion, swede, carrots, tinned black-eyed beans, tinned kidney beans.

This is a nutritional, economical winter dish and the dumplings will undoubtedly become a firm family favourite.

**SERVES 4**

300 ml (10 fl oz) hot vegetable stock
150 g (5 oz) green or brown lentils
75 g (3 oz) self-raising flour
25 g (1 oz) vegetable suet
2 tablespoons chopped fresh coriander
1 tablespoon chopped fresh basil
75 g (3 oz) Cheddar, grated
3–4 tablespoons water
2 tablespoons olive oil
1 onion, roughly chopped
1 small swede, diced
2 carrots, diced
2 tablespoons tomato purée
2 tablespoons chopped fresh parsley
1 fresh bay leaf
1 tablespoon plain flour
350 ml (12 fl oz) red wine
120 ml (4 fl oz) water
400 g tin of black-eyed beans, drained
400 g tin of kidney beans, drained
Salt and freshly ground black pepper

Pour the stock into a pan, bring to the boil and stir in the lentils. Return to the boil, then cover and simmer for 15–20 minutes until the lentils are tender and the stock has been absorbed.

To make the dumplings, place the self-raising flour, suet, coriander, basil and Cheddar in large bowl. Gradually add enough water to mix to a soft dough. Shape into eight dumplings, then cover and set aside.

Heat the olive oil in a large pan and cook the onion, swede and carrots for 5 minutes. Stir in the tomato purée, parsley, bay leaf and flour. Gradually stir in the red wine followed by the water. Bring to the boil, then stir in the black-eyed beans and kidney beans, cover and simmer gently for 15–20 minutes until the vegetables are tender.

Cook the dumplings in a large pan of boiling water for 4–5 minutes until they puff up and rise to the surface of the pan. Remove with a slotted spoon.

Stir the cooked lentils into the cassoulet and add salt and pepper to taste. Ladle into serving bowls and arrange the dumplings on top. Serve immediately.

Dumplings can be flavoured with lots of exciting things. I like to add some chopped fresh herbs, a tablespoon of wholegrain mustard or handful of a grated cheese such as good mature Cheddar or Gruyère.

# Nutty Tofu Burgers and Oriental Stir-fry

Tofu is now known to be a valuable tool in the fight against osteoporosis and cancer. It is also free of fat and cholesterol, which makes it a miracle food, and it provides a healthy alternative source of protein. Tofu is fragile and needs a gentle hand, so I blended it for this recipe. If serving pieces of tofu, marinating it is highly effective.

Red pepper, cashew nuts, smoked tofu, long-grain rice, baby corn, mangetout, spring onions.

Pre-heat the oven to 220°C/425°F/Gas 7. Cook the rice in a pan of boiling salted water for 12–15 minutes until tender. Drain well.

Meanwhile, seed and quarter the pepper and place skin side up on a baking sheet and roast for 10–12 minutes until tender. Place in a plastic bag and set aside until cool enough to handle.

To make the burgers, heat a small non-stick frying-pan and cook the nuts over a high heat, shaking the pan continuously until golden brown. Place in a food processor with the tofu and garlic and whizz briefly until roughly chopped. Add the eggs, coriander and soy sauce and process again until the mixture binds together. With floured hands, shape into four even-sized burgers. Heat the oil in a heavy-based frying-pan and cook the burgers for 2–3 minutes on each side until golden brown; keep warm. These burgers are fragile.

Skin the pepper and place the flesh in a clean food processor. Blend until finely chopped, then pour in the olive oil and wine vinegar and continue to whizz until smooth; season to taste.

Heat the oil in a wok or large frying-pan and cook the spring onions, corn and mangetout for 1–2 minutes. Add the cooked rice, chives and soy sauce and stir-fry for a further 3–4 minutes until heated through.

To serve, arrange the burgers on a plate and drizzle round the red pepper sauce. Serve the rice in a separate bowl, garnished with the chervil and coriander.

The pepper sauce will keep in the fridge in a screw-top jar for a day. Just shake well before using. The burgers can be made a few hours ahead of time and reheated under a moderate grill – but remember, they are very delicate.

SERVES 2

FOR THE RED PEPPER SAUCE
1 red pepper, seeded and quartered
6 tablespoons olive oil
1 tablespoon white wine vinegar

FOR THE BURGERS
50 g (2 oz) cashew nuts
225 g (8 oz) smoked tofu
1 garlic clove, crushed
2 eggs
Handful of fresh coriander leaves
1 teaspoon soy sauce
1 tablespoon sunflower oil

FOR THE STIR-FRY
100 g (4 oz) long-grain rice
2 tablespoons olive oil
3 spring onions, chopped
200 g (7 oz) mixed baby corn and mangetout, diagonally sliced
3 tablespoons snipped fresh chives
3 tablespoons soy sauce
Salt and freshly ground black pepper
Fresh coriander and chervil leaves, to garnish

**PAUL RANKIN**
# A Taste of Tokyo

I love this type of light oriental food. The Japanese-style stir-fry contrasts beautifully in both flavour and texture with the crispy tofu and the rice-stuffed nori rolls. When making the nori rolls, try to find proper sushi rice – it has a sticky texture that makes the rolls easy to handle.

Japanese sushi rice, spring onions, firm tofu, carrot, cucumber, beansprouts, sheets of nori seaweed.

In a small pan, bring the stock to the boil. Add the rice and cook for 12–15 minutes until the liquid has been absorbed and the grains are tender. Chop the white part of the spring onions and stir into the rice.

Meanwhile, cut the tofu widthways into 2 cm (¾ in) slices. In a shallow bowl, mix together the flour, cornflour, ½ teaspoon of the ground ginger, ¼ teaspoon of the cayenne and a pinch of salt and pepper. In a separate bowl, whisk together the egg and milk. Dust the tofu with flour, dip into the egg mixture and then finally back into the flour to give a thick, even coating. Heat about 150 ml (5 fl oz) of vegetable oil in a wok and deep-fry the tofu slices for 2–3 minutes until golden brown. Drain on kitchen paper and keep warm.

Shred the reserved green part of the spring onions. Heat 2 tablespoons of vegetable oil in a separate wok and stir-fry the carrot, cucumber, beansprouts and spring onions for 2–3 minutes until tender but still firm; season with salt and pepper.

To make the nori rolls, soak the nori seaweed in cold water for 1–2 minutes until softened, then drain on kitchen paper. Lay the sheets on greaseproof paper and spoon the rice mixture across the centre of each piece. Using the paper, roll up to form neat cylindrical shapes.

To make the sauce, place the sesame oil, soy sauce, remaining ginger and cayenne, the honey and coriander in a small pan and cook gently for 2–3 minutes; season to taste.

To serve, spoon the stir-fry into the centre of a plate and arrange the tofu slices and nori rolls alternately around the edge. Drizzle over the sauce and garnish with chives.

Nori is laver seaweed that has been cooked, flattened and dried into thin sheets. It is perfect for wrapping around sushi but can also be used in oriental salads or noodle soups. Find it in specialist stores or larger supermarkets.

## SERVES 2

300 ml (10 fl oz) vegetable stock
50 g (2 oz) Japanese sushi rice
4 spring onions
250 g (9 oz) firm tofu
6 tablespoons self-raising flour
2 tablespoons cornflour
¾ teaspoon ground ginger
½ teaspoon cayenne
1 egg
2 tablespoons milk
Vegetable oil, for deep-frying
1 large carrot, cut into long matchsticks
¼ cucumber, cut into long matchsticks
200 g (7 oz) beansprouts
10 small sheets nori seaweed
2 tablespoons sesame oil
2 tablespoons soy sauce
1 teaspoon clear honey
1 teaspoon chopped fresh coriander
Salt and freshly ground black pepper
Snipped fresh chives, to garnish

# Thai Quorn Towers

Ready-rolled puff pastry, onion, carrots, celery, Thai red curry paste, Quorn chunks, root ginger, mushrooms, fresh spinach, sesame seeds.

This dish of Quorn in puff-pastry with Thai-spice vegetables is packed full of delightful flavours and looks stunningly appetizing on the plate.

**SERVES 4**

375 g pack of ready-rolled puff pastry
1 tablespoon milk
2 tablespoons olive oil
1 small onion, sliced
2 large carrots, cut into matchsticks
3 celery sticks, cut into matchsticks
1 teaspoon Thai red curry paste
1 teaspoon chopped fresh mint
Juice of ½ lemon
235 g pack of Quorn chunks
1 garlic clove, chopped
2.5 cm (1 in) piece of root ginger, finely chopped
2 tablespoons chopped fresh coriander
50 g (2 oz) mushrooms, sliced
175 g (6 oz) fresh spinach, stalks removed
100 ml (3½ fl oz) white wine
3 tablespoons double cream
2 tablespoons Greek yoghurt
Pinch of freshly grated nutmeg
1 teaspoon sesame seeds
Salt and freshly ground black pepper

Pre-heat the oven to 220°C/425°F/Gas 7. Cut four 13 cm (5 in) circles out of the pastry. Transfer to a baking sheet and brush with the milk. Bake for 8–10 minutes until golden brown and well risen.

Heat 1 tablespoon of the olive oil in a large frying-pan and cook the onion, carrots and celery for 3 minutes until softened. Stir in the curry paste, mint and lemon juice and simmer on a very low heat for 3–4 minutes. Season with salt and pepper.

Meanwhile, heat the remaining olive oil in a separate frying-pan. Add the Quorn, garlic, ginger and coriander and cook gently for 3–4 minutes. Stir in the mushrooms, spinach and wine and cook for a further 2 minutes until the spinach has wilted. Stir in the cream and yoghurt and add salt, pepper and nutmeg to taste.

To serve, spoon the Thai vegetables on to a plate. Halve the pastry rounds horizontally and sit the bases on the vegetables. Fill with the Quorn mixture and replace the lids. Sprinkle over the sesame seeds and serve immediately.

Quorn is a very useful meat substitute. It is made from a mushroom microprotein and has texture similar to that of chicken. It absorbs flavours well and is good for marinating. Now available in a variety of forms including mince and chunks.

PHIL VICKERY

# Cheesy Bake and Split-pea Cakes

Most people have forgotten about split peas but I enjoyed cooking with them – they're very tasty!

New potatoes, red pepper, onions, baby button mushrooms, paneer cheese, tinned yellow split peas, fresh brown breadcrumbs, fresh spinach.

Pre-heat the oven to 200°C/400°F/Gas 6. Cook the potatoes and mint leaves in a pan of boiling salted water for 10–12 minutes until tender.

Meanwhile, slice the pepper into 1 cm (½ in) wide rings discarding the seeds. Set the rings aside and roughly chop the top and bottom slices of the pepper.

Heat 1 tablespoon of the olive oil in a frying-pan and cook the onions and chopped pepper for 5 minutes until softened. Stir in the mustard and add salt and pepper to taste.

Gently heat the cream in a small pan, then stir in the mushrooms and cook for 3–4 minutes until tender. Stir in the snipped chives and add salt and pepper to taste.

Drain the potatoes and mint and transfer to an ovenproof dish. Spoon over half the onion mixture, then pour over the creamy mushrooms. Crumble the paneer on top, then bake in the oven for 8–10 minutes until golden brown.

Meanwhile, make the pea cakes. In a large bowl, mix together the split peas, the remaining onion mixture and the breadcrumbs. Stir in a little salt and pepper, then gradually add enough flour and egg to bind the mixture. Shape into four even-sized patties, then dust with a little flour.

Heat 2 tablespoons of the oil in a separate frying-pan and gently cook the patties for 5 minutes, turning once, until golden brown.

Heat 1 tablespoon of olive oil in a separate frying-pan and cook the pepper rings for 5 minutes until softened.

Heat 1 tablespoon of olive oil in a large pan and add the spinach. Cover and cook for 2–3 minutes, stirring occasionally until wilted. Drain well, then season with salt and pepper.

To serve, spoon the spinach on to a serving plate and arrange the pepper rings on top. Place the patties on the pepper rings and drizzle over the remaining tablespoon of olive oil. Serve with the paneer gratin.

Paneer is a soft cheese with a texture very similar to that of tofu. It is often used in Indian cookery and is the base of the Punjabi speciality Mattar Paneer. It can be found in the chill cabinets of large supermarkets but regular, full-fat curd cheese can be used as an alternative.

## SERVES 4

350 g (12 oz) new potatoes, halved
5 fresh mint leaves
1 red pepper
6 tablespoons olive oil
2 onions, chopped
2 teaspoons wholegrain mustard
300 ml (10 fl oz) double cream
150 g (5 oz) baby button mushrooms, quartered
Small bunch of fresh chives, snipped
175 g (6 oz) paneer cheese
420 g tin of yellow split peas, drained
100 g (4 oz) fresh brown breadcrumbs
25 g (1 oz) plain flour
1 egg, beaten
200 g (7 oz) fresh spinach, stalks removed
Salt and freshly ground black pepper

# Aubergine Towers with Bulgar Wheat

Bulgar wheat, aubergine, beef tomato, spring onions, baby corn, sesame seeds, Piri Piri sauce or other hot chilli sauce, Mozzarella.

This is a very stylish-looking dish that's deceptively simple to make.

## SERVES 2

100 g (4 oz) bulgar wheat
200 ml (7 fl oz) boiling water
2 eggs
5 tablespoons vegetable oil
1 small aubergine
4 tablespoons plain flour
100 g (4 oz) fresh white breadcrumbs
1 beef tomato, seeded and roughly chopped
1 tablespoon chopped fresh mint
1 tablespoon chopped fresh parsley
Juice of 1 lemon
1 bunch of spring onions, finely chopped, keeping white and green parts separate
100 g (4 oz) baby corn, halved lengthways
Pinch of ground ginger
2 teaspoons clear honey
vinegar
1 garlic clove, finely chopped
1 teaspoon sesame seeds
1 teaspoon coriander seeds
2 cardamom pods, crushed
2 teaspoons Piri Piri sauce or other hot chilli sauce
150 g (5 oz) Mozzarella, drained and sliced
Salt and freshly ground black pepper

Place the bulgar wheat in a large bowl and pour over the boiling water. Cover the bowl with clingfilm and set aside for 15 minutes so that grains can absorb the liquid.

Lightly beat together the eggs, 1 tablespoon of the oil and a pinch of salt. Cut the aubergine lengthways into three thick slices, then cut each slice on the diagonal to make two triangular shapes. Dip the aubergine slices into the flour, then egg and then breadcrumbs.

Heat 3 tablespoons of the oil in a heavy-based frying-pan and cook the aubergine slices for 5–6 minutes, turning once, until golden. Keep warm.

Stir the chopped tomato, mint, parsley, lemon juice, half of the green spring onions and plenty of salt and pepper into the bulgar wheat.

Heat the remaining 1 tablespoon of oil in a griddle pan or heavy-based frying-pan and cook the sweetcorn and white spring onions with the ground ginger for 3–4 minutes, stirring occasionally until tender and slightly charred.

In a small pan, whisk together the honey, vinegar, garlic, sesame seeds, coriander seeds, cardamom pods, Piri Piri sauce and the remaining green spring onions. Heat gently until warmed through, then strain the dressing into a small bowl.

To serve, spoon the bulgar wheat on to serving plates and place an aubergine slice on top. Arrange the Mozzarella slices over the aubergine, then top with another aubergine slice. Spoon the fried sweetcorn on top, then finish with the remaining aubergine slices. Spoon round the dressing and serve.

Bulgar wheat is a cracked wheat grain that has a lovely nutty flavour. It is generally available pre-cooked and only needs covering with boiling water so that it can absorb the liquid and fluff up. For a lovely Greek-style salad, stir in a couple of chopped tomatoes, a few cubes of feta cheese, some olive oil, lemon juice and chopped mint – delicious!

**PATRICK ANTHONY**

# Stuff Yourself with Mushrooms and Aubergines

Large mushrooms, long grain rice, onion, tinned chopped tomatoes, aubergine, Cheddar.

Here's a delicious combination of stuffed mushrooms with sautéed aubergines and cheese sauce, which makes a meat-free meal full of interesting flavours and textures – ideal accompanied by some well-dressed salad leaves and crusty Italian bread. If fresh basil leaves are unobtainable, then fresh marjoram may be substituted.

**SERVES 2**

4 large mushrooms, stalks removed and finely chopped
4 tablespoons olive oil, plus a little extra for brushing
100 g (4 oz) long-grain rice
½ onion, finely chopped
1 garlic clove, finely chopped
4 fresh basil leaves, chopped
4 tablespoons tinned chopped tomatoes
1 small aubergine

**FOR THE CHEESE SAUCE**
25 g (1 oz) butter
25 g (1 oz) plain flour
300 ml (10 fl oz) milk
60 g (2½ oz) Cheddar, diced
2 tablespoons double cream
Salt and freshly ground black pepper
Chopped fresh parsley, to garnish

Pre-heat the oven to 200°C/400°F/Gas 6. Brush the mushroom caps with a little oil and place in a lightly oiled ovenproof dish. Bake for 12–15 minutes until tender.

Meanwhile, cook the rice in a large pan of boiling, salted water for 12–15 minutes until the grains are tender, then drain well, cover and keep warm.

Meanwhile, heat 1 tablespoon of oil in a frying-pan and cook the onion, garlic and basil for 5 minutes until softened. Stir in the chopped mushroom stalks and tomatoes and cook for a further 2 minutes. Add salt and pepper to taste. Stir in the cooked rice and remove from the heat.

Cut the aubergine into small cubes. Heat the remaining oil in a separate frying-pan and stir-fry the aubergine over a high heat for 3–4 minutes until tender and golden; season to taste.

To make the sauce, melt the butter in a small pan, stir in the flour and cook for 1 minute. Gradually whisk in the milk and bring to the boil, stirring continuously to make a smooth, thickened sauce. Whisk in the cheese and cream, stirring until the cheese has melted. Season to taste.

To serve, place two mushrooms on each plate and spoon over the rice filling. Arrange the aubergine cubes around the edge of the plate, pour over the cheese sauce and garnish with the chopped parsley.

Aubergines do soak up a lot of oil during frying but to help control this, lightly brush with a little oil and bake, grill or stir-fry. For a zero fat (almost) option, try steaming or poaching the aubergine in a little stock.

# Lazy Lasagne with Spinach and Mushrooms

Here are two simply stunning ways to serve lasagne – one a traditional baked lasagne, the other a more unusual, but equally delicious, open version.

Fresh spinach, fresh lasagne sheets, onion, chestnut mushrooms, Parmesan, Mozzarella, tomato.

Pre-heat the oven to 220°C/425°F/Gas 7. Place two-thirds of the spinach in a pan with a little salt and pepper. Cover and cook gently for 3–4 minutes until wilted. Drain and keep warm.

Cook the pasta in a large pan of boiling water for 3–4 minutes until tender. Drain and cool under cold water.

Heat 2 tablespoons of the olive oil in a large frying-pan and cook the onion for 5 minutes until softened. Stir in the mushrooms and cook for a further 2–3 minutes. Season and then transfer half the mixture to a bowl and keep warm.

To make the baked lasagne, stir the cream, mustard and wine into the pan of onions and mushrooms and cook for 2 minutes. Set aside half the lasagne sheets for the open lasagne. Lay one sheet of cooked lasagne in a small, oiled ovenproof dish. Pour over half the mushroom sauce, scatter over a little Parmesan and top with a layer of spinach. Repeat the layers of lasagne, sauce, Parmesan and spinach and then top with the Mozzarella and any remaining Parmesan. Bake for 10–15 minutes until golden brown and piping hot.

To make the pesto for the open lasagne, put the basil and garlic in a food processor and whizz until finely chopped. Add the grated Parmesan and then, with the motor running, pour in 150 ml (5 fl oz) of the oil, processing until well blended. Season to taste.

Heat the remaining oil in a separate frying-pan and add the turmeric and parsley. Cook the remaining pasta sheets for 1–2 minutes, turning frequently until heated through.

To assemble the open lasagne, arrange a layer of fried pasta on a plate, pile on the reserved mushroom mixture and drizzle over half the pesto. Top with a final layer of pasta and pesto and garnish with the sliced tomato.

If you have dried lasagne to hand, cook it according to the packet instructions, then cool under cold water. When you are ready to assemble the lasagne, simply rinse the pasta in hot water first.

## SERVES 4

225 g (8 oz) fresh spinach, stalks removed
350 g (12 oz) fresh lasagne sheets
200 ml (7 fl oz) olive oil
½ onion, finely chopped
250 g (9 oz) chestnut mushrooms, sliced

### FOR THE BAKED LASAGNE
150 ml (5 fl oz) double cream
1 tablespoon wholegrain French mustard
100 ml (3½ fl oz) white wine
25 g (1 oz) Parmesan, grated
100 g (4 oz) Mozzarella, sliced

### FOR THE OPEN LASAGNE
Small handful of fresh basil leaves
2 garlic cloves
1 tablespoon grated Parmesan
1 teaspoon ground turmeric
2 tablespoons chopped fresh parsley
Salt and freshly ground black pepper
1 tomato, sliced, to garnish

vegetarian dishes

# Top Five Presentation Tips

It's very difficult to say just how important food presentation is. Each cook or diner has different priorities. Some aim for beautiful presentation and hardly notice the flavours and balance of the dish, while others belittle well-presented food as fussy and self-conscious ... it's pretty difficult to strike the right balance.

For me, taste and presentation are inextricably linked. I believe that the best produce, cooked well has a vibrancy and beauty that can't be beaten. Good produce makes presentation easy – you simply let it show itself. Although you are allowed to give it a little helping hand with the odd sprig of fresh herb, essentially you leave it alone.

Of course, there is the other more extravagant side to good presentation which tends to appear in restaurants, and on special occasions such as dinner parties and so on – I like to think of it as playfulness (especially on Ready Steady Cook) – it's all about having fun on the plate and making good use of your creative spirit. This kind of experimentation can go two ways and it may well lead to a great triumph or, on the flip-side, a total disaster ... so let me give you a few pointers to help you along the right path.

**Buy the Best Produce** Always buy the best produce you can afford. As I mentioned earlier, I believe this to be extremely important for many reasons. If, for example, you're trying to make a soggy piece of frozen fish look good, what a difficult task you are facing! The flesh is watery and mushy, which makes it hard to achieve a good colour when frying or grilling and it also tends to break up and lose its shape. And as for fruit and vegetables, compare the vibrancy of fresh herbs with their dried counterpart or a proud, green head of broccoli with a wilted, yellowing old stalk ... are you getting the picture? The quality of the produce you're working with makes all the difference because not only does fresh produce taste good, it looks a heck of a lot better too!

**Keep it Simple** For some people, good presentation and simplicity are a contradiction, but I firmly believe that keeping it simple is the key to attractive-looking food – show off the food itself, don't disguise it. The Japanese are probably the most presentation conscious in the world and the essence of their philosophy is simplicity.

Simplicity doesn't equal complacency but rather encourages care and thoughtfulness when it comes to preparing food. I know on Ready Steady Cook it often looks as though we chefs just throw the food on to the plate in a very spontaneous way, but believe me, we're thinking about how we'll present the dish all the way through the programme. And when it comes to crockery, always choose a simple plate to act as frame for your food, one that draws attention to rather than distracts from the food itself.

**Find a Theme** Find a theme and follow it through from the starter to the dessert. I can hear you all saying, 'Eh? What do you mean by that you crazy Irishman?' Well, let me explain.

Firstly, I find the colours of seasonal food very beautiful. Imagine all the subtle shades of, say, autumn combined. On our imaginary plate we have deep red cabbage, straw-coloured mushrooms and the rich brown of some sliced, roast game. A piece of bright and summery red pepper would look totally out of place here! Seasonal colours work well together; they're a naturally harmonious blend.

Your presentation themes are likely to be inspired by a particular style such as the intricacies of Japanese food, or perhaps you're aiming at a rustic Italian style. If you keep this picture in mind, you can focus your thoughts to help achieve the desired results by remembering things like the most appropriate garnish for your theme – tiny vegetable carvings for the ambitious Japanese dish or a lively sprig of fresh herbs for your rustic Italian supper.

**Let Go and Have a Bit of Fun** This is what I was talking about earlier – playfulness. Keep to the points already covered but make sure you give way to your own whims and ideas and let those creative juices flow. If you want to pile your food high, go ahead, and use whatever you have on hand to help you – cooking rings, pastry cutters, a section of plastic bottle or even a piece of drain pipe can make a super mould for stacking up salad leaves. Or go the opposite way and lay your food out flat so that the combination of elements forms a mosaic of colour and texture. Play with the colours, textures and shapes of the food you are presenting – it's great fun!

**Keep Up To Date with Current Trends** Read cookery books, magazines and of course watch TV programmes like Ready Steady Cook and you will be amazed how inspired you will feel by the sight of a beautiful dish (of food, of course!). One of the best ways to keep in touch with the latest presentation ideas is by leafing through some of the beautiful cook books available today. Never before have there been so many wonderful books and magazines with photos of gorgeous food – so take advantage of it! Look at the way that the food is being put together – the combination of colours, the beautiful simplicity of good produce, the texture, the themes, the style. And take care to read the recipes carefully; you'll often find clever little tips and tricks of the trade that you can put to good use. Practise presenting a dish until you've mastered it, then use the same techniques on other dishes and ingredients. With a little time and care, you'll soon be presenting beautiful food with your own individual flair. Good luck!

# Polenta Pick 'n' Mix

Instant polenta, Dolcelatte, red onion, chestnut mushrooms, avocado, natural cooked beetroot (not in vinegar).

This combination of small dishes – the hearty polenta with a vegetable gratin and an avocado salsa – go together to make a fun meal for two.

### SERVES 2

1 vegetable stock cube
550 ml (18 fl oz) white wine
375 g (13 oz) instant polenta
200 g (7 oz) Dolcelatte, crumbled
6 tablespoons olive oil, plus extra for greasing
1 red onion, finely chopped
1 garlic clove, finely chopped
250 g (9 oz) chestnut mushrooms, roughly chopped
1 tablespoon plain flour
150 ml (5 fl oz) red wine
1 avocado, skinned and stoned
4 natural cooked beetroot (not in vinegar)
4 tablespoons double cream
Juice of 1 lime
2 tablespoons chopped fresh coriander
Salt and freshly ground black pepper
Fresh basil leaves, to garnish

Place the stock cube and white wine in a pan and bring to the boil. Pour in the polenta and cook for 8 minutes, stirring continuously until smooth and thickened; season well to taste. Spoon half the polenta into an oiled Swiss roll tin, spreading it out to a thickness of about 2 cm (¾ in), then place in the fridge to set. Stir half the Dolcelatte into the remaining polenta, cover and keep warm.

Heat 1 tablespoon of olive oil in a small pan and cook the onion and garlic for 5 minutes until softened. Stir in the mushrooms and cook for 2 minutes, then add the flour and cook for a further 1 minute. Gradually stir in the red wine, then bring to the boil and simmer rapidly for 2–3 minutes until smooth and thickened. Season to taste and keep warm.

To make the gratin, slice half the avocado and beetroot and layer in a small heatproof dish. Pour over the cream and sprinkle with the remaining cheese. Place under a pre-heated grill for 6–7 minutes until bubbling and golden.

Meanwhile, make the salsa. Dice the remaining avocado and beetroot and mix with 2 tablespoons of olive oil, the lime juice and coriander, and season to taste.

Cut the set polenta into triangles. Heat the remaining oil in a griddle pan or heavy-based frying-pan and cook the triangles for 2 minutes on each side until crisp and golden.

To serve, spoon the cheesy polenta onto a serving plate, top with the mushrooms and garnish with basil leaves. Arrange the griddled polenta triangles around the salsa and serve with the gratin.

Try not to prepare the avocado too far in advance as the flesh will discolour; a squeeze of lemon or lime juice will help prevent this.

# Juicy Ratatouille Pancakes

This dish captures all that is lovely about 'sunshine' ingredients – a real flavour pack!
The use of griddled vegetables adds texture as well as colour.

Dried lemon grass, onion, red pepper, courgettes, sweet potato, tinned artichoke hearts, tinned chopped tomatoes.

To make the pancake batter beat the eggs in a large bowl, then gradually add the flour and then milk to make a smooth batter. Stir in the spices and a little salt and pepper, cover and place in the fridge for 10 minutes, to rest.

Heat 2 tablespoons of the olive oil in a heavy-based frying-pan and cook the onion, garlic, red pepper, diced courgette and diced sweet potato for 2–3 minutes until beginning to soften. Stir in the artichokes, all the juice from the can of chopped tomatoes and half of the flesh, 1 tablespoon of tomato purée, 100 ml (3½ fl oz) of water, the chopped coriander and parsley and plenty of salt and pepper. Simmer for 5–7 minutes until the vegetables are tender.

Meanwhile, brush the sliced courgette and sweet potato with a little olive oil and season with salt and pepper. Heat a griddle pan or heavy-based frying pan and cook the vegetables for 3 minutes. Mix together the remaining tomato purée and the wine, turn the vegetables and pour in the wine mixture. Cook for a further 3 minutes until the vegetables are tender and golden and the liquid has been absorbed.

Heat a lightly oiled 20 cm (8 in) frying-pan. Stir the chopped basil into the batter, then pour 2–3 tablespoons of the mixture into the hot pan, swirling to coat the base. Cook for 1–2 minutes on each side, then repeat to make eight pancakes in total.

Mix together the remaining tomato flesh and the remaining olive oil. Fill the pancakes with the ratatouille and fold over. Place on a serving plate and arrange the griddled vegetables around the edge. Drizzle over the tomato sauce, garnish with the parsley sprigs and serve.

Canned artichoke hearts in brine are available in most supermarkets, though of course in the summer make good use of the abundant fresh globe artichokes around.

## SERVES 4

2 eggs
100 g (4 oz) plain flour
300 ml (10 fl oz) milk
¼ teaspoon ground cumin
¼ teaspoon chilli powder
¼ teaspoon paprika
¼ teaspoon dried lemon grass
3–4 tablespoons olive oil
1 onion, chopped
1 garlic clove, crushed
1 red pepper, seeded and diced
2 courgettes, 1 diced, 1 sliced diagonally
1 sweet potato, ½ diced, ½ sliced
400 g tin of artichoke hearts, drained and roughly diced
400 g tin of chopped tomatoes
2 tablespoons tomato purée
1 tablespoon chopped fresh coriander
1 tablespoon chopped fresh parsley
Vegetable oil, for frying
1 tablespoon white wine
2 tablespoons chopped fresh basil
Salt and freshly ground black pepper
Fresh parsley sprigs, to garnish

**BRIAN TURNER**

# Yorkshire Puddings Deluxe

This dish of Yorkshire puddings with mixed vegetables, pepper and potato cakes and onion gravy should be served as traditional Yorkshire puddings – before roast beef.

 Onion, plum tomatoes, courgettes, button mushrooms, potatoes, red pepper.

Pre-heat the oven to 220°C/425°F/Gas 7. Brush a four-hole Yorkshire pudding tin with a little oil and place in the oven. Whisk together the eggs and milk, then sift over 100 g (4 oz) flour and a pinch of salt and beat together to make a smooth batter. Pour the batter into the hot pudding tin and bake for 15–20 minutes until well risen and golden brown.

Meanwhile, heat the remaining oil in a frying-pan and cook the onion for 8–10 minutes until softened and golden brown.

Melt 15 g (½ oz) of the butter in a separate frying-pan and cook the tomatoes for 2 minutes. Stir in the courgettes, mushrooms and garlic and cook gently for 8 minutes until tender. Season to taste.

Put the potato and pepper in a sieve and push with a wooden spoon to squeeze out any liquid. Turn into a bowl and mix with 1 tablespoon of flour and plenty of salt and pepper. Melt 15 g (½ oz) of butter in a separate heavy-based frying-pan and add the potato mixture, patting it out to a thickness of about 1 cm (½ in). Cook for 8–10 minutes, stirring occasionally to break up the mixture, until tender and golden.

Meanwhile, place the stock in a pan and bring to the boil. Stir in the wine, fried onions, remaining butter and the parsley and simmer rapidly for 5 minutes. Season to taste.

Place four 7.5 cm (3 in) ring moulds in the centre of a large plate, spoon in the potato mixture, then lift off the rings. Place a Yorkshire pudding on top of each potato round and spoon on the vegetable mixture. Pour round the onion gravy and serve immediately.

Pre-cooked beef dripping is the best fat to cook Yorkshire puddings in – it gives them a tremendous flavour, though if you're cooking for vegetarians, you'd better stick to olive oil.

SERVES 4

2 tablespoons olive oil
4 eggs
250 ml (8 fl oz) milk
100 g (4 oz) plain flour, plus 1 tablespoon
Pinch of salt
1 large onion, thinly sliced
50 g (2 oz) butter
2 plum tomatoes, quartered
2 courgettes, cut into 2.5 cm (1 in) lengths
100 g (4 oz) button mushrooms, quartered
1 garlic clove, crushed
350 g (12 oz) potatoes, finely grated
1 red pepper, seeded and finely chopped
600 ml (1 pint) vegetable stock
4 tablespoons white wine
2 tablespoons chopped fresh parsley
Salt and freshly ground black pepper

**NICK NAIRN**

# Summer Vegetable Stack with Chunky Chutney

Spring onions, yellow tomatoes, aubergine, red pepper, yellow pepper, courgettes.

This is a lovely summery dish that you can make with a variety of seasonal vegetables such as courgettes and asparagus. The tomato chutney can be made up to a week in advance.

**SERVES 2**

6 tablespoons olive oil
1 bunch of spring onions, thinly sliced
3 yellow tomatoes, diced
1½ tablespoons clear honey
Grated rind and juice of ½ lime
2 tablespoons snipped fresh chives
6 tablespoons sunflower oil
1 aubergine, cut lengthways into 5 mm (¼ in) thick slices
1 red pepper
1 yellow pepper
1 teaspoon ground coriander
Juice of 1 lime
1 tablespoon chopped fresh coriander
2 courgettes, cut lengthways into 5 mm (¼ in) thick slices
Juice of ½ lemon
Salt and freshly ground black pepper

To make the chutney, heat 1 tablespoon of the olive oil in a small pan and cook the white part of the spring onions for 1 minute; reserve the green part. Stir the tomatoes, 1 tablespoon of honey and the lime rind and juice into the pan and cook gently for 5–6 minutes until soft and pulpy. Season with salt and pepper and stir in 1 tablespoon of chives.

Sprinkle the aubergine slices with salt and set aside for 10 minutes. Rinse the aubergine in cold water, then pat dry. Heat 5 tablespoons of sunflower oil in a large frying-pan and cook the aubergine slices for 2–3 minutes on each side until tender and golden brown.

Meanwhile, cook the peppers under a pre-heated grill for 8–10 minutes, turning frequently until the skin is blackened and blistered. Cover with a clean tea towel and leave to cool for 2 minutes. Skin, seed and quarter the peppers. Finely dice 1 red and 1 yellow pepper quarter; set the whole pieces aside.

To make the pepper sauce, heat the remaining olive oil in a small pan and add the reserved green part of the spring onions, the ground coriander, lime juice, fresh coriander and diced peppers. Cook gently for 5 minutes, then stir in the remaining honey and chives and season to taste.

Heat the remaining sunflower oil in a large frying-pan and cook the courgette slices for 1 minute on each side until golden. Squeeze in the lemon juice and season to taste. To serve, fold the aubergine and courgette slices in half widthways and layer up with the peppers, placing a teaspoon of chutney between each layer. Pour round the sauce.

I always cover peppers with a piece of clingfilm straight after they've been roasted as the steam helps lift off the skin. Once peeled, the peppers can be stored for a few days in a jar topped up with olive oil – for extra flavour add a crushed garlic clove and a sprig of thyme.

**AINSLEY HARRIOTT**

# Cheesy Broccoli Soufflés with Mushroom Croûtes

Cooking this all in twenty minutes for **Ready Steady Cook** was really pushing it but you'll have a lot more time than I did and the success of the end result will give you bags of confidence and of course, lots of happy diners.

Parmesan, broccoli florets, Gruyère, button mushrooms, French bread.

Pre-heat the oven to 180°C/350°F/Gas 4. Grease six ramekins with a little oil then sprinkle ½ tablespoon of Parmesan into each ramekin, shaking to coat the insides.

In a pan, gently heat the milk; do not allow to boil. Melt the butter in a separate pan, then stir in the flour and cook for 1 minute, stirring continuously. Whisk in the hot milk and slowly bring to the boil, beating until smooth and thickened; season with salt, pepper and nutmeg.

Cook the broccoli in a large pan of boiling salted water for 3–5 minutes until tender; drain well and mash roughly with a fork. Stir the broccoli, egg yolks and Gruyère into the white sauce. In a separate bowl, whisk the egg whites until they form soft peaks, then carefully fold into the sauce. Divide between the six ramekins, sprinkle over the remaining Parmesan and bake for 15 minutes until risen and golden.

Meanwhile, make the croûtes. Melt the butter in a frying-pan and cook the mushrooms for 5 minutes until tender and golden. Stir in the cream and parsley and add salt and pepper to taste; keep warm. Heat the olive oil in a separate frying pan and cook the bread for 2–3 minutes on each side until golden brown; drain on kitchen paper.

To make the Hollandaise sauce, place the white-wine vinegar, water and peppercorns in a small pan and simmer rapidly until the liquid is reduced to about 1 tablespoon. Transfer to food processor and whizz until the peppercorns are finely chopped. Add the egg yolks then, with the motor running, very slowly pour in the melted butter to form a smooth, glossy sauce; season to taste.

To serve, arrange the croûtes on a plate and spoon over the mushrooms; top with the Hollandaise. Remove the soufflés from the oven and serve both dishes immediately.

Serve your soufflés on a warm plate immediately they come out of the oven. Make sure the rim of the soufflé dish is wiped clean once filled, so you get a nice even rise.

## SERVES 6 AS A STARTER

2 tablespoons olive oil
4 tablespoons grated Parmesan
275 ml (9 fl oz) milk
25 g (1 oz) butter
25 g (1 oz) plain flour
¼ teaspoon freshly grated nutmeg
225 g (8 oz) broccoli florets, cut into small pieces
3 eggs, separated
150 g (5 oz) Gruyère, grated

### FOR THE CROÛTES
25 g (1 oz) butter
225 g (8 oz) button mushrooms, sliced
5 tablespoons double cream
1 tablespoon chopped fresh parsley
3–4 tablespoons olive oil
6 slices French bread, sliced diagonally

### FOR THE SAUCE
2 tablespoons white-wine vinegar
3 tablespoons water
10 peppercorns
3 egg yolks
175 g (6 oz) unsalted butter, melted
Salt and freshly ground black pepper

**vegetarian dishes**

**ROSS BURDEN**

# Perfect Pumpkin Ravioli with Sage Butter

Mixed candied peel, flaked almonds, Ricotta, pumpkin, Parmesan.

Cappellacci or pumpkin ravioli are a speciality of Bologna and although time-consuming are a most impressive dish for a special occasion.

**SERVES 2**

225 g (8 oz) plain flour
2 eggs

**FOR THE FILLING**
¼ pumpkin, seeded and chopped
1 tablespoon mixed candied peel
50 g (2 oz) flaked almonds
250 g (9 oz) Ricotta
1 egg yolk
1 egg, lightly beaten

**FOR THE SAUCE**
100 g (4 oz) butter
2 tablespoons chopped fresh sage
Pinch of freshly grated nutmeg

1 tablespoon freshly grated Parmesan, to serve
Salt and freshly ground black pepper
Fresh sage leaves, to garnish

To make the pasta, place the flour, eggs and a pinch of salt in a food processor and blend until the mixture resembles fine breadcrumbs. Turn the mixture out on to a floured surface and bring together to form a firm dough. Knead lightly, cover with clingfilm and set aside to rest, ideally for an hour to allow the flour to relax. This makes rolling the pasta much easier.

Chop the pumpkin into 2.5 cm (1 in) pieces and simmer for about eight minutes. Meanwhile, in a clean food processor, whizz together the mixed peel and almonds until finely chopped. Add the Ricotta, pumpkin and egg yolk and blend until smooth. Season with salt and pepper.

Divide the pasta dough into four. Using a pasta machine or rolling pin, roll each piece of dough out thinly to a rectangle roughly measuring 25 x 8 cm (10 x 3 in).

Lay the pasta on a work surface and put 2 teaspoons of the pumpkin mixture in even rows on two of the sheets. Brush round the filling with beaten egg. Place the other two sheets on top and press round each mound of filling to seal well. Using a 5 cm (2 in) pastry cutter, cut round each mound. This mixture makes about 20 ravioli. Bring a pan of salted water to the boil and cook the pasta for 3 minutes.

Meanwhile, to make the sauce, melt the butter in a small pan. When foaming, stir in the sage and nutmeg. Drain the ravioli and toss in the butter. Transfer to a plate and dust with parmesan. Pour over the sage sauce, sprinkle with Parmesan and garnish with the fresh sage.

Cooked sweet potato can be used instead of ravioli. The ravioli can be blanched in boiling water for one minute, dunked into cold water and, oiled, kept in the fridge for a couple of hours. Dunk again to reheat, but too long in the fridge and they will go slimey!

# Melting Mozzarella Bruschetta

Aubergine, Mozzarella, pitted black olives, tomato.

A wonderful, warming bruschetta with great melt-in-the-mouth textures. After all, not much beats melting Mozzarella for customer contentment!

### SERVES 2

### FOR THE TAPENADE
100 g (4 oz) stoned black olives
1 garlic clove, roughly chopped
1½ tablespoons olive oil
2 tablespoons chopped fresh coriander
½ teaspoon Dijon mustard
1 teaspoon balsamic vinegar

### FOR THE BRUSCHETTA
4 tablespoons olive oil
2 x 1 cm (½ in) thick slices white country-style bread, crusts removed
1 garlic clove, halved
1 small aubergine, cut into 1 cm (½ in) thick slices
100 g (4 oz) Mozzarella, drained
Salt and freshly ground black pepper

### TO SERVE
1 large tomato, sliced
3–4 fresh basil leaves
1 tablespoon olive oil
Freshly ground black pepper

Begin by making the tapenade. Place the olives, garlic, oil, coriander, mustard and vinegar in a food processor and whizz together until smooth. Add salt and pepper to taste.

Heat 1 tablespoon of the olive oil in a large frying-pan and cook the bread for 2–3 minutes on each side until crisp and golden. Remove from the pan and rub the fried bread with the cut surface of the garlic.

Heat the remaining oil in the same frying-pan and cook the aubergine slices for 3–4 minutes on each side until tender and golden brown, then drain on kitchen paper.

Spread the tapenade on the bruschetta and overlap the aubergine slices on top. Arrange the Mozzarella on top of the aubergine and place under a pre-heated grill for 2–3 minutes until the cheese has melted.

To serve, place the bruschetta on two plates and garnish with the sliced tomatoes and basil leaves. Drizzle with a little olive oil and sprinkle with a good grinding of black pepper. Serve warm.

When frying bread, use dripping or bacon fat rather than oil for better flavour. Alternatively, for your favourite 'eggy' bread (dipped in milk, rather than beaten egg), use clarified butter.

**PATRICK ANTHONY**

# Mushroom Pasta with a Twist

A mixed bag of market-fresh vegetables and a few handy store-cupboard flavour-makers creates a colourful and lively pasta dish for two.

Pasta twists, large flat mushrooms, onion, small fennel bulb, beef tomato, baby carrots, sweetcorn, green beans.

Cook the pasta in a large pan of boiling salted water for 10 minutes until tender.

Slice the mushrooms in half horizontally. Heat 2 tablespoons of sunflower oil in a large frying-pan and cook the mushroom slices for 5 minutes, turning once until tender. Keep warm.

Meanwhile, heat 2 tablespoons of sunflower oil in a separate pan and cook the onion and fennel for 3 minutes. Stir in the tomato, soy sauce, Tabasco sauce, Worcestershire sauce, cream and seasoning and continue to cook gently for 5 minutes until the vegetables are tender.

Meanwhile, heat the remaining sunflower oil in a separate wok or large frying-pan and stir-fry the carrots, sweetcorn and green beans over a high heat for 4 minutes until tender but still crisp. Stir in the sesame oil and snipped chives and season to taste.

Drain the pasta well and toss with the olive oil.

To serve, place the mushroom slices on serving plates and spoon over the pasta. Pour over the cream sauce and sprinkle with the coriander. Spoon the stir-fried vegetables around the edge of the plate and garnish with the fresh chives and lime slices.

If you'd like to use fresh pasta for quicker cooking, then penne (quills) would be the best alternative choice.

### SERVES 2

175 g (6 oz) pasta twists
2 large flat mushrooms, stalks removed
6 tablespoons sunflower oil
1 onion, chopped
1 small fennel bulb, chopped
1 beef tomato, chopped
1 teaspoon light soy sauce
Few drops of Tabasco sauce
Few drops of Worcestershire sauce
150 ml (5 fl oz) double cream
75 g (3 oz) baby carrots, cut into 1 cm (½ in) thick slices
75 g (3 oz) sweetcorn
75 g (3 oz) green beans, trimmed
1 teaspoon sesame oil
1 tablespoon snipped fresh chives
1 tablespoon olive oil
Salt and freshly ground black pepper
Chopped fresh coriander, chives and lime slices, to garnish

**RICHARD CAWLEY**

# Autumn Vegetable Pie

Quick and easy, this elegant dish will prove a popular main course with vegetarians and carnivores alike, and takes full advantage of the fact that most supermarkets now sell an excellent selection of fresh herbs all year round.

 Baby new potatoes, carrots, broccoli, cheese such as Gruyère or Cheddar.

Pre-heat the oven to 200°C/400°F/Gas 6. To make the pastry, place the flour, butter and salt in a food processor and whizz until the mixture resembles fine breadcrumbs. Add the egg yolk and enough water to blend to a firm dough.

On a floured surface, roll out the pastry to a thickness of about 5 mm (¼ in). Using a small, sharp knife, cut out eight large leaf shapes. Transfer to a baking sheet, brush with beaten egg and bake for 10–15 minutes until golden brown.

To make the filling, cook the potatoes in a large pan of boiling salted water for 10–12 minutes until tender. Remove the potatoes from the pan with a slotted spoon and add the carrots and broccoli. Cook for 3–4 minutes until tender.

Meanwhile, melt the butter in a large pan, then stir in the flour and cook for 1 minute. Gradually beat in the milk to make a smooth sauce. Stir in the cheese, chopped herbs and salt and pepper to taste. Add the cooked vegetables, stir well and cook for a few minutes until the cheese has melted and the vegetables are heated through.

To serve, spoon the saucy vegetables on to four serving plates and top each plate with two pastry leaves. Garnish with the chives.

 If you wrap freshly made pastry in clingfilm, or simply place it in a plastic bag and allow it to 'rest' in the fridge for about 30 minutes, it will be easier to roll out and much less likely to shrink during cooking.

SERVES 4

200 g (7 oz) plain flour
100 g (4 oz) butter
Pinch of salt
1 small egg yolk
5 tablespoons water
1 egg, beaten

FOR THE FILLING
250 g (9 oz) baby new potatoes, halved lengthways
3 carrots, sliced
350 g (12 oz) broccoli, cut into small florets
50 g (2 oz) butter
2 tablespoons plain flour
450 ml (15 fl oz) milk
225 g (8 oz) cheese such as Gruyère or Cheddar, grated
1 tablespoon chopped fresh dill
1 tablespoon snipped fresh chives
Salt and freshly ground black pepper
Snipped fresh chives, to garnish

**ANTONY WORRALL THOMPSON**

# Let's Twist Again

Fusilli (pasta spirals), aubergine, plum tomatoes.

A quick and easy vegetarian pasta with a little kick. You'll love the interesting use of aubergine in the tomato sauce.

### SERVES 2

225 g (8 oz) fusilli (pasta spirals)
5 tablespoons olive oil
1 small aubergine, cut into 1 cm (½ in) thick slices
1 garlic clove, chopped
½ teaspoon hot chilli powder
225 g (8 oz) plum tomatoes, skinned and diced
2 teaspoons balsamic vinegar
1 tablespoon chopped fresh basil
Salt and freshly ground black pepper
Fresh basil sprigs, to garnish

Cook the pasta in a large pan of boiling water for 10–12 minutes until tender but still firm.

Meanwhile, make the sauce. Heat 3 tablespoons of the olive oil in a large frying-pan and cook the aubergine slices for 3–4 minutes on each side until tender and golden brown. Drain on kitchen paper, then cut each slice into quarters.

Heat 1 tablespoon of the remaining oil in the same frying-pan and cook the garlic and chilli powder for 1 minute, without colouring. Stir in the tomatoes, vinegar and basil and gently heat through. Stir in the cooked aubergine and season to taste.

To serve, drain the pasta well and toss with the remaining tablespoon of olive oil. Stir in the aubergine sauce and transfer to serving bowls. Garnish with the basil sprigs and serve.

When draining pasta, it will not get sticky if placed in a warm colander. Avoid any pasta product that lists 'disodium phosphate' on the label. It is a chemical softening agent that helps pasta cook faster. Use dried pasta for better results – with fresh pasta it is hard to achieve *al dente* quality.

**PAUL RANKIN**
# Oriental Express

These delicious nibbles – vegetable kebabs, tempura and omelette spirals – are all Japanese-inspired. Meat-eaters can add chicken or prawns, if desired.

Small cauliflower, courgette, red pepper, carrot, spring onions, spinach, fresh root ginger.

To make the kebabs, thread half the cauliflower florets, courgette, pepper and carrot slices on to two skewers. Mix together the honey, mustard and soy sauce and brush over the kebabs. Cook under a hot grill for 10 minutes, turning occasionally until tender and golden.

To make the tempura, lightly whisk together the egg yolks, 2 tablespoons of the flour and water to make a lumpy batter. Dust the reserved cauliflower, courgette, pepper, carrot and spring onions with the remaining flour. Dip the floured vegetables into the batter and deep-fry in hot oil for 2–4 minutes until crisp and golden. Drain on kitchen paper.

To make the omelette spirals, mix together the spinach, pepper, courgette, carrot, spring onions, ginger and coriander in a glass bowl. Season well. Cover with microwave film and cook at PL9/High for 3–4 minutes or, alternatively, steam until tender. Drain well.

Heat the oil in a small frying-pan and pour in the beaten eggs. Cook for 2 minutes on each side until golden and set. Slide the omelette out on to a board, spoon the vegetables over the top and roll up. Cut diagonally into 2.5 cm (1 in) thick slices.

To make the dip, stir together the soy sauce, honey, coriander and ginger. Pour into a small serving bowl.

To serve, place the dip in the centre of a large platter and arrange the vegetable kebabs, tempura and omelette spirals around the dip.

The secret to successful tempura lies in four key points:

1 Don't overmix the batter, simply stir a few times with a fork – it should be lumpy.
2 Use ice-cold water.
3 Make the batter in small batches and use immediately.
4 The oil must be at the correct temperature (165–170°C/330–340°F) so the filling will be cooked by the time the batter has crisped and browned.

SERVES 2

FOR THE KEBABS AND TEMPURA
1 small cauliflower, cut into florets
1 courgette, thickly sliced diagonally
½ red pepper, thickly sliced diagonally
1 carrot, thickly sliced diagonally
1 tablespoon clear honey
1 tablespoon Dijon mustard
1 tablespoon soy sauce
2 egg yolks
4 tablespoons plain flour
5 tablespoons ice-cold water
3 spring onions
Sunflower oil, for deep-frying

FOR THE OMELETTE SPIRALS
100 g (4 oz) fresh spinach stalks removed
½ red pepper, seeded and diced
1 courgette, grated
1 carrot, grated
3 spring onions, finely chopped
1 cm (½ in) piece of root ginger, finely chopped
1 tablespoon chopped fresh coriander
1 teaspoon vegetable oil
3 eggs, beaten

FOR THE DIP
2 tablespoons soy sauce
1 tablespoon clear honey
½ tablespoon chopped fresh coriander
1 cm (½ in) piece of root ginger, finely chopped
Salt and freshly ground black pepper

# FISH AND SHELLFISH

RICHARD CAWLEY

# Posh Fish and Chips

New potatoes, piece of root ginger, salmon tail, mangetout.

Everyone loves really good, fresh fish fried golden brown in a crisp, light batter. This foolproof batter is based on a genuine recipe used in Yorkshire fish and chip shops (where the best fish and chips come from!). And now that farmed salmon is often no more expensive than cod or haddock, it adds that unmistakable touch of class to a once humble, everyday dish.

### SERVES 2

Sunflower oil, for deep frying
25 g (1 oz) butter
100 g (4 oz) new potatoes, diced
1 garlic clove, chopped
4 tablespoons plain flour
1 teaspoon bicarbonate of soda
100 ml (3½ fl oz) cold water
2.5 cm (1 in) piece of root ginger, grated
Juice of 1 lemon
275 g (10 oz) salmon tail, cut into 1 cm (½ in) wide strips
150 g (5 oz) mangetout
Salt and freshly ground black pepper
Fresh parsley sprigs, to garnish

Heat 1 tablespoon of oil and the butter in a frying-pan. Add the diced potatoes and cook for 7–8 minutes until beginning to turn golden. Add the garlic and cook for a further for 3–4 minutes until the potatoes are tender.

Meanwhile, make the batter. Place the flour and bicarbonate of soda in a bowl and whisk in the cold water to make a smooth batter. Stir in the ginger, lemon juice and a little salt. Dip the salmon strips into the batter then deep-fry in hot sunflower oil for 3–4 minutes until crisp and golden brown. Drain on kitchen paper.

Heat a little oil in a wok or heavy-based frying-pan and stir-fry the mangetout for 1 minute until tender but still firm.

To serve, pile the garlic potatoes on to a plate and spoon over the mangetout. Arrange the crispy salmon strips on top and garnish with the parsley sprigs.

It is often the air bubbles in successful batters that make them light and crisp. Some batters, like those made with yeast, need to rest for a period before use. Speedy batters have an acidic element such as lemon juice, which reacts with the bicarbonate of soda to make bubbles, and are best mixed at the last minute and used immediately, while still foaming.

**ANTONY WORRALL THOMPSON**

# Squids in!

This squid-ink risotto is a fabulous dish – it's about time supermarkets started selling squid ink sachets.

Risotto rice, packet squid ink, squid, cos lettuce, tomatoes, Parmesan.

Pre-heat the oven to 200°C/400°F/Gas 6. Melt the butter in a large pan, stir in the rice and cook for 1 minute. Stir in the squid ink and, keeping the heat fairly high, gradually add the hot stock a ladle at a time, stirring until the liquid is absorbed and the rice is tender and creamy. This will take about 20 minutes.

Place the bread cubes in a large bowl and toss with the olive oil. Scatter on to a non-stick baking sheet and cook in the oven for about 8 minutes, turning occasionally until crisp and golden brown.

Meanwhile, make the salad dressing. Place the garlic, Worcestershire sauce, egg yolk, Parmesan and lemon juice in a food processor and whizz until smooth. Add the olive oil and mustard and blend again. Season to taste and set aside.

Score the inside of the squid flesh in a lattice pattern. Brush the squid with a little oil and cook in a hot griddle pan or heavy-based frying pan for 30 seconds on each side. Season with salt and pepper.

To serve, spoon the risotto into a large serving bowl and top with the griddled squid. Toss together the lettuce, tomatoes, salad dressing and croûtons and transfer to a serving bowl. Sprinkle over the snipped chives.

 To make sure your squid is tender, there are two cooking times. Either grill or boil for no more than 1 minute, or simmer for about 1–1 ½ hours. Any of the times in between will make the squid tough. Squid ink is available in sachets from the fishmonger.

## SERVES 2

50 g (2 oz) butter
225 g (8 oz) risotto rice
1 packet of squid ink
600 ml (1 pint) hot vegetable stock
2 slices of country-style bread cut into 2 cm (¾ in) cubes
4 tablespoons olive oil
225 g (8 oz) clean fresh squid, halved lengthways
1 cos lettuce, roughly torn into bite-sized pieces
2 tomatoes, skinned, seeded and quartered

## FOR THE SALAD DRESSING

2 garlic cloves
1 teaspoon Worcestershire sauce
1 egg yolk
40 g (1½ oz) Parmesan, grated
Juice of 1 lemon
2 tablespoons olive oil
1 teaspoon wholegrain mustard
Salt and freshly ground black pepper
Snipped fresh chives, to garnish

# Flavours of the East

The most wonderful thing about Asian food is the intensity of flavour of each constituent ingredient. The full palette that makes up Eastern food may be many things – but it is never shy. A day in an Asian market is a riot of colour, flavour and theatre, more so than in any other area of the world. The simplest of dishes can be transformed by the use or addition of the following six ingredients which, to me, are the essence of the Asian flavour: clean, light and pure. All these items are best bought in Asian supermarkets in Asian (large) quantities; the tiny prices will astound you.

**Chilli** This, in fact, came to the East from the New World but has been taken as Asia's own. Indian chillies are usually mild and make a fantastic roadside snack when dipped in chickpea batter and deep-fried as pakoras. The Szechwan dish of beef stir-fried with whole dried red chillies is entirely different in style from the minced green chillies in a Thai *tom yam*, but they share the clear and fiery flavour that both cuisines favour. Chillies are also great for hangovers in that they take one's mind away from the head to the mouth by releasing endorphins. The vast diversity of types of chilli ranges from mild to very hot; as a rough guide, the smaller or narrower the chilli, the hotter it will be. The flavour of chilli can be ameliorated by the use of sugar, such as in *nam prik*, Thai sweet chilli sauce, but however it is used, do always mind your eyes! Wash your hands and equipment thoroughly after preparation.

**Soy Sauce** This has been used for hundreds of years by the Chinese and Japanese, who make the pungent sauce from fermented beans and salt. The finest sauces are to be found in Japan; dipping wafer-thin slices of freshly delivered tuna in soy muddied with wasabi paste is about as fine an experience as one can cope with at six a.m. Tofu is made from cooked soya beans which are liquidized to a milk, then resolidified by using calcium sulphate. It has been found to be very useful in preventing osteoporosis and breast cancer. Marinated in fresh ginger and sautéed it gives the lie to the idea that it is a bland dish. The sweet *ketjap manis* of Indonesia is

a highly viscous version which makes an ideal gravy browning as well as making a fantastic marinade for skinless chicken thighs with ginger wine and hoisin, a sauce made with plum sauce and more soy.

**Coriander** Chinese parsley, dhania and cilantro are all names for the pungent herb beloved throughout Asia. The fresh, clear taste of a Thai shredded vegetable salad or *yam* and the mellow richness of Indian coriander chicken both owe everything to this flavoursome herb. The seeds are also highly aromatic with a distinct orangey flavour, and they are used in Thai, Indian and Vietnamese spice mixes. Gin production also uses huge quantities of coriander seeds. The roots are never wasted and are a major flavouring in Vietnamese pork ball soup. Coriander is great added to salsa verde and has affinities with papaya, mango and fish. Now available in large supermarkets as a bushy and verdant bunch, the best comes from Thai shops and is much more delicate, particularly appropriate if it is to be used raw as a welcome addition to a salad.

**Lime** This fruit is used in much the same way as lemon but tastes green! Ideal in a 'g&t', think of a chair and the sun setting over the Taj. Fish is an especially good partner; in ceviche; squeezed over a grilled fillet; or in a salsa. Limes are pickled whole in India and form a curry accompaniment packed with vitamin C. Lime juice is used in dressings for salads, especially green papaya salad in Vietnam and Thailand. The shredded leaves make a fragrant addition to salads and coconut-based curries. Essential with fresh papaya, limes also make a great *tarte au citron* with a difference. Prawns, minced and moulded around lemon grass skewers are fantastic barbecued and, served with wedges of lime, bring back memories of Singapore.

**Mangoes** These are the best fruit in the world, and as a breakfast provide a cleansing enzyme boost for the day. As a fresh fruit they can be used in many ways, and dried and ground they become *amchur* powder which is used in place of citrus for sourness in Indian curries. Whole, they are best eaten with the hands, but they can also be highly sophisticated, especially as a topping for tarts in the manner of Hanoi patissiers. Mango chutneys, either fresh and green or mellow and sweetened, would be an unthinkable omission at an Indian meal, their fruitiness perfectly partnering any spicy food. I often buy boxes going cheap at the market and create pulp which freezes wonderfully and which I can then use as the base for quick fools or ice-creams.

**Toasted sesame oil** This pungent brown oil is like a perfume, used sparingly to add fragrance and delicacy to many dishes in the East. Made from toasted seeds, ground and washed, it is high in zinc and is highly economical due to the tiny amounts required. As an ingredient in marinades for barbecue food it has no equal. Splashed into soups or stir-fries, it lifts the most prosaic to the ethereal. A must for everyone's store cupboard.

# Fried Plaice with Pea and Mint Mash

Potato, frozen peas, shallots, button mushrooms, muscovado sugar, plaice fillets.

For this recipe, I filleted a whole plaice myself but any fishmonger would be happy to do it for you.

**SERVES 2**

1 large potato, diced
225 g (8 oz) frozen peas
1 tablespoon chopped fresh mint
25 g (1 oz) butter

**FOR THE SAUCE**

25 g (1 oz) butter
4 shallots
150 ml (5 fl oz) white wine
75 g (3 oz) button mushrooms, sliced
1 tablespoon chopped fresh tarragon
Grated rind of 1 lemon
Grated rind of 1 lime
3 tablespoons double cream

**FOR THE FISH**

3 tablespoons plain flour
25 g (1 oz) light muscovado sugar
½ teaspoon ground cumin
4 skinless, boneless plaice fillets
1 tablespoon olive oil
15 g (½ oz) butter
Juice of ½ lemon
Salt and freshly ground black pepper

Plaice has a lovely, delicate flavour, but any flat fish would be suitable for this recipe. Try it with lemon or Dover sole, turbot, halibut or brill.

Cook the potato in a large pan of boiling salted water for 10 minutes. Add the peas and mint and cook for a further 3–4 minutes until softened. Drain well, then return to the pan. Mash together, then add the butter and season with salt and pepper to taste; cover and keep warm.

Meanwhile, make the sauce. Place the butter, shallots, wine, mushrooms, tarragon and citrus rind in a pan. Bring to the boil and simmer gently for 6 minutes. Stir in the cream and continue to simmer gently for a few minutes until slightly thickened.

To cook the fish, mix together the flour, sugar, cumin and a little salt and pepper. Lightly score the flesh of each plaice fillet and coat in the seasoned flour, shaking off the excess. Heat the oil and butter in a large heavy-based frying-pan and cook the fish for 3–4 minutes on each side until golden. Squeeze over the lemon juice and remove from the heat.

To serve, place a 7.5 cm (3 in) ring mould in the centre of two plates and fill with the mash. Place the shallots on either side of the mash and pour round the sauce. Remove the moulds and place two fried plaice fillets on top of each pile of mash.

**NICK NAIRN**

# Swanky Salmon

This dish of seared salmon with sweet potato and rocket and tomato salad is my all-time favourite way to cook this succulent fish. For more top salmon ideas, turn to my special pages on the subject (page 70). *Illustrated on page 46.*

 Sweet potato, tomatoes, onion, salmon fillet, rocket leaves.

Heat the sunflower oil in a deep frying-pan. Wash the sweet potato matchsticks in cold water to remove any excess starch, then dry carefully. Deep-fry the matchsticks in batches until crisp and golden. Drain on kitchen paper.

To make the sauce, heat together the wine, half the onion, half the mustard and the vegetable stock in a small pan. Bring to the boil and simmer gently for 5 minutes, then stir in the cream and half the lemon juice. Remove from the heat and gradually whisk in the butter to give a rich, glossy sauce. Add the chopped chervil and then, using an electric hand blender, whizz until smooth. Add salt and pepper to taste.

Quarter the tomatoes then halve each piece widthways. Place in a bowl with the remaining chopped onion and mustard, 1 tablespoon of olive oil and the vinegar. Toss well together.

Heat 1 tablespoon of olive oil in a large frying-pan set over a high heat. When the pan is very hot, cook the salmon for 1 minute only. Remove with a spatula, then season with salt, pepper and a squeeze of lemon juice.

To serve, toss the rocket leaves in with the tomato salad and pile into the centre of a plate. Arrange the salmon strips on top of the salad and pile the sweet potato sticks on top. Pour round the sauce and garnish with the chervil sprigs.

 Rocket has a strong pepper flavour and can be a bit of an acquired taste. However, if you persevere you'll soon come to love its unique flavour – it's wonderful as a salad with some grated Parmesan, a splash of olive oil, a drizzle of balsamic vinegar and plenty of freshly ground black pepper – yum! As an alternative for this recipe, use baby spinach leaves.

## SERVES 2

600 ml (1 pint) sunflower oil
1 large sweet potato, about 275 g (10 oz), cut into fine matchsticks
250 ml (8 fl oz) white wine
1 small onion, finely chopped
1 teaspoon Dijon mustard
120 ml (4 fl oz) vegetable stock
2 tablespoons double cream
Juice of 1 lemon
25 g (1 oz) unsalted butter, diced
2 tablespoons chopped fresh chervil
4 tomatoes
2 tablespoons olive oil
1 tablespoon balsamic vinegar
250 g (9 oz) skinless, boneless salmon fillet, cut into 1 cm (½ in) wide strips
25 g (1 oz) rocket leaves
Salt and freshly ground white pepper
Fresh chervil sprigs, to garnish

# Wham Bam Spaghetti Clam

Spring onions, tinned chopped tomatoes, broccoli, fennel bulb, fresh spaghetti, tinned clams.

This is a version of one of my favourite dishes, which I normally make with mussels. In fact, I first did it for Masterchef in 1993 and the ingredients in this bag were ideal. The freshness of the ingredients is the key.

### SERVES 2

8 spring onions
4 tablespoons olive oil
400 g tin of chopped tomatoes, drained
150 ml (5 fl oz) water
1 teaspoon ground turmeric
50 g (2 oz) butter
250 g (9 oz) broccoli, cut into small florets
1 fennel bulb, cut into small pieces
1 tablespoon chopped fresh sage
225 g (8 oz) fresh spaghetti
290 g tin of clams, drained
Salt and freshly ground black pepper
Fresh herbs, such as basil and chervil, to garnish

Cut the green ends off the spring onions and thinly slice them lengthways into shreds. Place the shreds in a bowl of iced water and set aside to curl. Finely slice the remainder of the spring onions.

To make the tomato sauce, heat 2 tablespoons of the olive oil in a pan and gently cook the spring onions for 2–3 minutes until softened. Sieve the chopped tomatoes into the pan, pushing them through the mesh with a metal spoon. Stir in the water and bring to the boil. Stir in the turmeric and half the butter. Whizz with a hand blender until smooth, then season with salt and pepper and keep warm.

Heat the remaining olive oil in a frying-pan and cook the broccoli and fennel over a high heat for 3–4 minutes, until tender. Remove with a slotted spoon and drain on kitchen paper.

Meanwhile, heat the remaining butter in a separate frying-pan and cook the sage leaves for 1 minute until crisp. Drain on kitchen paper.

Cook the spaghetti in a large pan of boiling salted water for 3–4 minutes until tender. Drain well, then toss with the sage butter.

To serve, transfer the spaghetti to a large soup plate. Scatter the fried vegetables and the clams over the spaghetti. Top with the tomato sauce and garnish with the spring onion curls and fresh herbs.

Tinned clams are an ideal store-cupboard ingredient. They are so convenient, and enliven any meal. Try them in risottos, as an additional ingredient in a home-made fish soup, or even in a salad of green leaves served with a lemony dressing and crusty French bread.

**RICHARD CAWLEY**

# Coconut Crab and Spicy Stir-fry

Dressed crab, fresh coconut, carrots, potato, green beans, red chilli, spring onions.

Although this recipe can easily be extended to serve as many as you wish, it makes a lovely treat of a meal for one – perfect for when you feel like pampering yourself, with the added advantage that it can be prepared and cooked in minutes.

**SERVES 1**

1 dressed crab
2 tablespoons chopped fresh coriander
¼ fresh coconut, grated
½ teaspoon dried ginger
1 tablespoon double cream
1–2 tablespoons olive oil
2 garlic cloves
1 red chilli, seeded and chopped
3 carrots, cut into batons
1 potato, cut into batons
50 g (2 oz) green beans
1 bunch of spring onions, finely chopped
2 tablespoons chopped fresh mint
Salt and freshly ground black pepper
Lime wedge, to garnish

Pre-heat the oven to 200°C/400°F/Gas 6. Scoop the crab meat out of the shell and mix with half the coriander, the coconut, ginger and double cream. Add salt and pepper to taste, then pile the mixture back into the shell. Bake for 8–10 minutes until golden brown.

Heat the olive oil in a wok or large frying-pan and stir-fry the garlic and chilli for 1 minute. Add the carrot, potato and beans and cook for a further 3–4 minutes. Stir in the spring onions, mint and remaining coriander and season with salt and pepper. Continue to cook for a few minutes until the vegetables are tender.

To serve, pile the vegetables on to a plate and place the filled crab on top. Garnish with the lime wedge and serve immediately.

The fresher the crab the better the flavour, so try and buy your crab from a reputable fishmonger with a good turnover. If buying from a supermarket, however, do not be afraid to ask how fresh the crab is and when it was dressed. You don't want to buy something that has been on 'display' for several days.

**BRIAN TURNER**

# Cods Wallop

This is a very different version of my usual fish and chips. The cod is served with sautéed sweet potatoes and a spicy stir-fry of red peppers with yellow oyster mushrooms, elevating a humble dish to an exotic feast.

Cod fillet, red chilli, sweet potato, red onion, red pepper, yellow oyster mushrooms.

Skin the fish and halve the fillet. Place the skin and any trimmings in a pan with the wine and water. Bring to the boil and simmer gently for 10 minutes.

Meanwhile, make the batter. Lightly whisk together the eggs, cream, dill and a little salt and pepper, then set aside to rest.

Melt 15 g (½ oz) butter in a small pan and cook the chilli for 30 seconds. Set aside.

Parboil the sweet potato in a large pan of boiling salted water for 5 minutes. Drain well. Heat 1 tablespoon of sunflower oil and 25 g (1 oz) of butter in a separate frying-pan and cook the sweet potato for 5 minutes, turning frequently until golden brown.

Meanwhile, heat 25 g (1 oz) of the butter in a wok or large frying-pan and cook the garlic, red onion and pepper for 5 minutes until softened. Stir in the mushrooms and fried chilli and cook for a further 2–3 minutes until tender. Season to taste.

Heat 1 tablespoon of oil in a separate, large heavy-based frying pan. Coat the fish in the seasoned flour then dip in the batter. Shallow-fry for 2–3 minutes on each side until golden brown and just cooked through. Remove with a spatula and drain on kitchen paper.

Strain the fish stock into a clean pan and simmer rapidly until reduced by half. Stir in the wine vinegar and season to taste.

To serve, spoon the pepper mixture into the centre of a plate and place the fish on top. Arrange the sweet potatoes around the edge and spoon over the sauce.

To skin the fish, firmly hold a sharp knife at a 45 degree angle to the skin, then pull the fish, from the tail end, using a side-to-side motion to release the flesh.

**SERVES 2**

350 g (12 oz) cod fillet
3 tablespoons white wine
200 ml (7 fl oz) water
2 eggs
1 tablespoon double cream
1 tablespoon chopped fresh dill
65 g (2½ oz) butter
1 red chilli, seeded and finely chopped
1 large sweet potato, about 450 g (1 lb), diced
2 tablespoons sunflower oil
1 garlic clove, finely chopped
1 red onion, finely chopped
1 red pepper, seeded and diced
150 g (5 oz) yellow oyster mushrooms, halved if large
50 g (2 oz) seasoned plain flour
½ tablespoon white wine vinegar
Salt and freshly ground black pepper

# Dreamy Bream with Langoustines

Potato, tomatoes, langoustines, onion, yellow pepper, samphire, black bream.

This recipe for black bream with samphire and langoustines makes a very sophisticated dish that's out to impress. Ask your greengrocer to get hold of the herb samphire for you or substitute with young, tender asparagus spears.

### SERVES 2

1 teaspoon ground turmeric
1 large potato cut into 2 cm (¾ in) slices
11 tablespoons olive oil
2 tomatoes, quartered
1 teaspoon salt
3 teaspoons caster sugar
2 teaspoons balsamic vinegar
6 langoustines
1 teaspoon tomato purée
1 onion, thinly sliced
1 yellow pepper, seeded and cut into 2 cm (¾ in) pieces
Sunflower oil, for deep-frying
1 tablespoon snipped fresh chives
2 teaspoons white wine vinegar
100 g (4 oz) samphire
1 x 350 g (12 oz) black bream, filleted
4 tablespoons seasoned plain flour
Salt and freshly ground black pepper

There are so many different names for the same shellfish. Here's my quick guide to small crustaceans:
Langoustine, Dublin Bay Prawn and scampi are like mini lobsters and have a delicious firm textured flesh. Crayfish are fresh water shellfish which can still be found in the streams and rivers of Britain. They are a shorter, stockier looking version of the langoustine with crab-like claws. Prawns vary enormously in shape and colour from tiny brown shrimps to the succulent tiger prawns from South-east Asia.

Pre-heat the oven to 220°C/425°F/Gas 7. Place the turmeric and potato slices in a large pan of boiling salted water and cook for 10–12 minutes until tender.

Meanwhile, heat 2 tablespoons of the olive oil in an ovenproof frying-pan, add the tomatoes and cook for 1–2 minutes. Sprinkle over the salt and 2 teaspoons of the sugar. Roast in the oven for 7–8 minutes until tender, then drizzle over the balsamic vinegar, cover and keep warm.

Meanwhile, cook the langoustines in a large pan of boiling water for 1 minute, then drain well. Remove the heads, peel the tails and set aside. Place the heads and tomato purée in a small pan and heat gently, crushing the heads with the back of a wooden spoon to release all the flavours. Pour in 6 tablespoons of olive oil and warm through very gently for 3–4 minutes. Remove from the heat and set aside to infuse.

Place the onion in a sieve, sprinkle liberally with salt and set aside. Heat 1 tablespoon of the olive oil in a separate pan and cook the pepper pieces skin-side down over a high heat for 3–4 minutes until the skin begins to char. Remove and keep warm.

Rinse the onions and pat dry on kitchen paper. Deep-fry in hot sunflower oil for 2–3 minutes until crisp and golden brown. Drain on kitchen paper.

Strain the langoustine oil through a piece of muslin or a clean j-cloth and stir in the chives, white wine vinegar, remaining sugar and salt and pepper to taste, then set aside.

Blanch the samphire in a large pan of boiling water for 1–2 minutes until tender but still firm. Drain well and toss with 1 tablespoon of olive oil.

Dust the fish fillets with the seasoned flour. Heat the remaining tablespoon of olive oil in a separate frying-pan and cook the fish over a high heat for 1–2 minutes on each side until golden and just cooked through.

To serve, arrange the tomatoes and langoustine tails around the edge of two plates. Place the samphire in the centre of the plates and arrange the turmeric-potatoes on top. Place the fish fillets on the potatoes and drizzle round the langoustine dressing. Garnish with the crispy onions and serve immediately.

**KEVIN WOODFORD**

# Lobster in Creamy Wine Sauce with Herb Rice

Shallots, long-grain rice, whole lobster.

Lobster is expensive, but as a treat on a special occasion, it's well worth the money. If you are reluctant to dissect the lobster yourself, ask your fishmonger to do it for you.

### SERVES 2

1 tablespoon olive oil
1 shallot, finely chopped
100 g (4 oz) long-grain rice
2 tablespoons chopped fresh dill
1 tablespoon chopped fresh coriander
1 tablespoon chopped fresh basil
1 vegetable stock cube dissolved in 900 ml (1½ pints) hot water

### FOR THE LOBSTER

1 cooked lobster
25 g (1 oz) butter
1 shallot, finely chopped
1 garlic clove, crushed
85 ml (3 fl oz) white wine
2 teaspoons Dijon mustard
3 tablespoons double cream
1–2 teaspoons fresh lemon juice
1 egg yolk
Salt and freshly ground black pepper
Lemon wedges, to garnish

Heat the oil in a heavy-based frying-pan and cook the shallot for 1 minute. Add the rice, stirring to coat in the oil. Mix together the herbs and stir 2 tablespoons of the mixture into the pan. Pour in the hot stock, bring to the boil and simmer gently for 12–15 minutes until the rice has absorbed the stock and the grains are tender. Spoon the rice into two large, buttered ramekins.

Meanwhile, prepare the lobster. Lay the lobster on its back and cut it in half from head to tail. Discard the stomach sac and intestinal tract. Scoop out all the tail meat from both halves of the body, including the green meat. Cut off the legs and claws; crack open and remove the meat. Wash and dry the body shells.

Melt the butter in a small pan and cook the shallot, garlic and remaining chopped herbs for 3–4 minutes until softened. Pour in the wine and bring to the boil. Stir in the mustard and cream and simmer gently for 3 minutes. Add the lobster flesh and stir in the lemon juice and salt and pepper to taste. Stir in the egg yolk and heat through very gently; do not allow the mixture to boil.

To serve, spoon the lobster flesh and sauce back into the half shells. Turn the rice out on to serving plates and garnish with the lemon wedges.

It's very important not to overcook the lobster flesh as it becomes tough when subjected to too much heat.

**ALASTAIR LITTLE**

# Sensational Salmon

Hollandaise is one of my favourite classic French sauces and it works beautifully with this dish of fresh salmon with courgette and broccoli.

Salmon fillet pieces, onion, potatoes, red chilli, broccoli, courgettes.

Sprinkle the skin side of the salmon with plenty of salt and set aside.

Heat the olive oil a large frying-pan and cook the onion for 5 minutes until softened, then remove from the heat. Add the sliced potatoes to the pan and cook for 6–7 minutes until tender and golden. Stir in the chilli, softened onion and add salt and pepper to taste.

To make the Hollandaise, place the eggs, lemon juice and a pinch of salt in a food processor or liquidizer and whizz until well blended. With the motor running, slowly pour in the butter to make a foamy sauce.

Cook the broccoli in a pan of boiling salted water for 1 minute. Add the courgettes and cook for a further 1–2 minutes until just tender. Drain well, return to the pan and cover to keep warm.

Heat a large non-stick frying-pan over a high heat and cook the salmon skin-side down for 5 minutes until the skin is crispy and slightly charred. Turn and cook for a further 2–3 minutes, until just cooked.

To serve, put the salmon in the centre of a serving plate. Arrange the broccoli and courgettes around the salmon and drizzle the Hollandaise sauce over the vegetables. Garnish with flatleaf parsley and chives. Spoon the potatoes into a separate dish and serve any remaining Hollandaise sauce separately.

## SERVES 2

2 x 150 g (5 oz) salmon fillets
1 tablespoon olive oil
1 onion, sliced
350 g (12 oz) potatoes, sliced
1 red chilli, seeded and finely chopped
2 eggs
Juice of 1½ lemons
225 g (8 oz) butter, melted
225 g (8 oz) broccoli, broken into small florets
2 courgettes, cut diagonally into 1 cm (½ in) thick slices
Salt and freshly ground black pepper
Fresh flatleaf parsley and chives, to garnish

Salting the skin of fish and poultry draws out the moisture so that when it is cooked quickly in an intense heat, the skin crisps up beautifully – this is also the key to good, crunchy pork crackling.

**fish and shellfish**

## ANTONY WORRALL THOMPSON

# Hot and Spicy Pronto Prawns

This colourful stir-fry of tiger prawns and vegetables served with couscous is incredibly quick and easy to prepare. Mix and match the vegetables to suit your taste or try adding other fruit such as pineapple.

 Couscous, ginger purée, Chinese leaf lettuce, red pepper, spring onions, mango, tiger prawns.

Place the couscous in a large heatproof bowl and pour over the boiling water. Set aside for 8 minutes for the grains to absorb the liquid. Stir in half the garlic, the cumin, coriander, chives, mint and salt and pepper. Place two 9 cm (3½ in) heart-shaped pastry cutters on a heatproof plate and spoon in the mixture, pressing down well. Sit the plate inside a steamer and cook for 10 minutes.

Meanwhile, heat the olive oil in a wok or large frying-pan and stir-fry the remaining garlic, the ginger, Chinese leaf, three-quarters of the pepper, the spring onions, mango and Tabasco sauce over a high heat for 3–4 minutes. Add the prawns and cook for a further 2–3 minutes until they turn pink and the vegetables are tender but still firm. Season to taste.

To serve, carefully transfer the couscous hearts to two plates and spoon round the prawn stir-fry. Garnish with the reserved red pepper and coriander sprigs.

 Green Tabasco sauce is made from Jalapeño chillies and has a far milder flavour than the original fiery red sauce. It can be used generously to add flavour to all kinds of dishes such as stir-fries and salsas.

### SERVES 2

100 g (4 oz) couscous
300 ml (10 fl oz) boiling water
2 garlic cloves, crushed
½ teaspoon ground cumin
1 tablespoon chopped fresh coriander
1 tablespoon chopped fresh chives
1 tablespoon chopped fresh mint
2 tablespoons olive oil
2 teaspoons ginger purée
½ Chinese leaf lettuce, finely shredded
½ red pepper, finely chopped
1 bunch of spring onions, thinly sliced
1 small mango, skinned, stoned and diced
1 teaspoon green Tabasco sauce
10 raw tiger prawns, peeled
Salt and freshly ground black pepper
Fresh coriander sprigs, to garnish

# Tickled Trout and Beetroot Crisps

Fennel bulb, trout fillets, beetroot, cucumber, red onion, red pepper, tomatoes.

If you think of trout as a fiddly, bone-packed fish then you'll be pleased to know that good quality, skinless, boneless, Scottish trout fillets are now widely available in supermarkets. This very modern dish cleverly pairs the delicate flavour of the fish with juicy, firm-textured fennel and sweet beetroot crisps.

### SERVES 2

Sunflower oil, for deep-frying
1 fennel bulb, quartered
1 garlic clove, finely chopped
2 x 75 g (3 oz) skinless, boneless trout fillets
6 tablespoons white wine
2 teaspoons lemon juice
4 tablespoons hot vegetable stock
2 small beetroot, very thinly sliced

### FOR THE SAUCE

½ cucumber, peeled, seeded and roughly chopped
1 red onion, roughly chopped
1 red pepper, seeded and roughly chopped
4 tomatoes, roughly chopped
3 garlic cloves, finely chopped
5 tablespoons chopped fresh basil
150 ml (5 fl oz) olive oil
1 tablespoon tomato ketchup
5 tablespoons hot vegetable stock

### FOR THE CROUTES

2 slices white bread
2 tablespoon olive oil
Salt and freshly ground black pepper
Fresh chives, to garnish

Pre-heat the oven to 200°C/400°F/Gas 6. Half-fill a deep frying-pan with sunflower oil and heat gently.

Heat 2 tablespoons of sunflower oil in an ovenproof frying-pan and cook the fennel and garlic for 3–4 minutes, turning occasionally until browned.

Twist the trout fillets and place them in a small, oiled ovenproof dish. Drizzle over 2 tablespoons of the wine, the lemon juice and plenty of salt and pepper. Place in the oven for 7–8 minutes until the fish is just cooked. Pour the remaining wine and the stock into the fennel pan with a little salt and pepper and place in the oven for 15 minutes until tender.

Deep-fry the beetroot slices in batches for 1–2 minutes until crisp and ruffled. Drain well on kitchen paper.

Meanwhile, make the sauce. Place the cucumber, red onion, red pepper, tomatoes, garlic, basil, olive oil, tomato ketchup, stock and plenty of salt in a food processor and pulse to form a coarse sauce.

To make the croûtes, stamp one 9 cm (3½ in) circle out of each slice of bread. Heat the olive oil in large heavy-based frying-pan and cook the bread for 2–3 minutes on each side until golden brown.

To serve, spoon the sauce on to two plates and place a croûte in the centre of each. Place a trout fillet on each croûte and scatter over the beetroot crisps. Arrange the fennel around the edge of the plate and garnish with the chives.

 Fennel has a lovely, delicate aniseed flavour and can be cooked in many ways. When braising, as in this dish, it really improves the flavour if you first fry the quarters in olive oil to brown all over. If you are using slices, make sure you keep a piece of the root intact, otherwise the slices will fall apart in the pan. I also really like fennel when cooked into a purée or grated finely and served raw as part of a crunchy salad.

# Exotic Raspberry Kedgeree

I would never normally pair raspberries with haddock but they were both in my shopping bag for this programme and luckily enough, the dish worked remarkably well.

Long-grain rice, Arbroath Smokies, cucumber, onion, raspberries.

Pre-heat the oven to 230°C/450°F/Gas 8. Cook the rice in a large pan of boiling salted water for 10–12 minutes until tender. Drain well.

Place the Arbroath Smokies on a baking sheet and dot with 15 g (½ oz) of butter. Season with pepper and place in the oven for 6–8 minutes until heated through.

Remove strips of the skin from each piece of cucumber with a canelle knife and scoop out the seeds with a teaspoon or melon baller. Cook in a large pan of boiling water for 2 minutes. Cool under cold water and drain well.

Heat the oil in a frying-pan and cook the onion for 5 minutes until softened. Stir in the juice of 1 orange, 1 lemon and 1 lime, the honey and soy sauce. Simmer for 3–4 minutes until syrupy, then stir in the citrus rind and vinegar and simmer for a further 2–3 minutes. Stir in the raspberries and cook for 1 minute. Season to taste and remove from the heat.

Melt 50 g (2 oz) of the butter in a separate frying-pan and stir in the rice. Season the eggs, pour over the rice and cook for 1–2 minutes, stirring continuously until the egg has just set.

Melt the remaining butter in a small pan and stir in the reserved lime juice.

To serve, spoon the rice into the centre of a serving plate. Cut the Arbroath Smokies into 5 cm (2 in) pieces and pile on top of the rice. Arrange the cucumber pieces round the rice and spoon the raspberry compote into the hollows in each piece. Drizzle over the lime butter and serve immediately.

Arbroath Smokies are hot-smoked, small haddock from Scotland. They have an exceptional flavour and only need heating through gently – take care not to overcook.

SERVES 2

100 g (4 oz) long-grain rice
2 x 100 g (4 oz) Arbroath Smokies
90 g (3½ oz) butter
1 cucumber, cut into 4 cm (1½ in) lengths
1 tablespoon olive oil
1 onion, finely chopped
Juice of 1 orange
Juice of 1 lemon
Juice of 1½ limes
2 tablespoons clear honey
2 teaspoons soy sauce
Grated rind of 1 orange
Grated rind of 1 lime
Grated rind of ½ lemon
1 teaspoon red wine vinegar
225 g (8 oz) raspberries
2 eggs, lightly beaten
Salt and freshly ground black pepper

**AINSLEY HARRIOTT**

# Hot and Herby Mackerel with Sautéed Sweet Potatoes

Sweet potato, whole mackerel, red chillies, iceberg lettuce.

If you're looking to eat healthily, you really can't beat mackerel. We're constantly being told to include more fish in our diets, especially the oily varieties like mackerel and herring, so accompanied here by delicious, sautéed sweet potato, it makes the perfect meal.

**SERVES 2**

3 spring onions to garnish
225 g (8 oz) sweet potato, peeled and sliced lengthways
1 fresh coriander sprig
4 tablespoons olive oil
2 whole mackerel, cleaned and scaled
4 red chillies, seeded and finely chopped
Grated rind and juice of 1 lemon
2 tablespoons chopped fresh coriander
1 tablespoon chopped fresh parsley
1 teaspoon chopped fresh mint
1 teaspoon chopped fresh basil
1 teaspoon chopped fresh tarragon
2 garlic cloves, finely chopped
½ iceberg lettuce, finely shredded
Salt and freshly ground black pepper
2 red chillies, seeded and sliced

To make the spring onion garnish, slit the ends of the spring onions lengthways without cutting them right through, and put them in iced water until the ends curl.

Cook the sweet potato slices and coriander sprig in a large pan of boiling salted water for 6–8 minutes until tender. Drain the potato and pat dry with kitchen paper; discard the coriander. Heat 2 tablespoons of the olive oil in a heavy-based frying-pan and cook the sweet potato for 2–3 minutes on each side until golden brown.

Meanwhile, prepare the mackerel. Cut four diagonal slits, 1 cm (½ in) deep, in each side of the mackerel. Mix together the chopped chillies, lemon rind and juice, herbs, garlic and plenty of salt and pepper. Stuff three-quarters of the mixture into the mackerel cavities. Heat the remaining oil in a separate frying-pan, add the mackerel, cover and cook for 6 minutes, turning once. Remove from the pan and cook under a pre-heated grill for a further 3–4 minutes, turning occasionally until well browned and cooked through.

Toss together the shredded lettuce and remaining herb mixture.

To serve, pile the lettuce on to a large serving plate and top with a layer of sweet potato slices. Arrange the mackerel on the sweet potato and spoon over the cooking juices. Garnish with the spring onion tassels and sliced chillies.

Fresh mackerel is available all year round and is very economical. It can also be bought in a whole load of other ways including pickled, both hot and cold smoked, often with a cracked pepper coating.

# Tilapia and Sweet-potato Gnocchi

Sweet potatoes, tilapia fish, spring onions, leek, crème fraîche.

Gnocchi seem to have the same mystery attached to them as soufflés, i.e. 'these are far too difficult to make', but once again, there's nothing further from the truth. Once you've made them following this recipe, they'll be on the menu time and again at meal times. Go on and try them, you won't be disappointed.

### SERVES 2

2 sweet potatoes, diced
150 g (5 oz) plain flour
1 egg, beaten
1 tablespoon chopped fresh rosemary
1 x 350 g (12 oz) tilapia
2 spring onions, finely chopped
1 tablespoon chopped fresh coriander
3 tablespoons olive oil
1 leek, thinly sliced
1 garlic clove, finely chopped
2 tablespoons crème fraîche
Salt and freshly ground black pepper
3 spring onions, thinly sliced, to garnish

To make the gnocchi, cook the sweet potatoes in a large pan of boiling salted water for 10 minutes until softened. Drain the potatoes well and roughly mash. Mix with the flour, beaten egg, rosemary and plenty of salt and pepper. On a floured surface, roll the gnocchi mixture out into a long sausage. Cut the sausage into 1 cm (½ in) lengths. Cook the gnocchi in a large pan of boiling salted water for 3–4 minutes until they float to the surface of the water. Drain well.

Meanwhile, diagonally score the fish on both sides. Season the slashes with salt and pepper, then pack them with the spring onions and coriander. Heat 2 tablespoons of olive oil in a heavy-based frying-pan and cook the fish for 7–8 minutes, turning once, until cooked through and golden brown.

Heat the remaining oil in a large frying-pan and cook the leek and garlic for 5 minutes, until softened. Season with salt and pepper and stir in the crème fraîche and the gnocchi. Cook gently until heated through.

To serve, pile the gnocchi in a serving plate and arrange the tilapia on top. Garnish with the spring onion slices.

Make sure that your gnocchi mixture is soft but firm – if it is too sloppy you can always add a little more flour, but remember to season well. A piping bag helps as you can actually slice the gnocchi straight into the boiling water.

Tilapia is a very popular tropical sea fish with a firm flesh and clean, fresh flavour. Other good tropical fish suitable for this dish would include snapper and parrot fish, or if you prefer sea fish, try red mullet.

**ALASTAIR LITTLE**
# Hungry for Haddock

I like cooking with haddock. It has a delicious flavour and flakes into good, firm chunks. Because of its lovely flavour, I like to cook it quite simply and find that it eats very well topped with potatoes and served with a light creamy sauce full of fresh herbs like the one I've made here.

Haddock fillet, potatoes, frozen peas, onion, tomatoes.

Pre-heat the oven to 200°C/400°F/Gas 6. Place the haddock on a greased baking sheet and season with salt and pepper. Arrange the potato slices, slightly overlapping on top of the fish. Dot with half of the butter and sprinkle with a little salt and pepper. Bake for 12–15 minutes until tender and golden.

Cook the peas in pan of boiling salted water for 3 minutes until tender. Drain well.

Place the wine and chopped onion in a small pan. Bring to the boil and simmer for 5 minutes until the onion is tender. Add the peas, cream, chopped tomatoes and remaining butter and gently warm through. Stir in the chopped herbs and season with salt and pepper.

To serve, arrange the fish in the centre of a large plate and spoon round the creamy sauce. Garnish with lemon wedges.

Fresh dill is traditionally paired with fish. It has a delicate aniseed flavour and should never be cooked for more than a minute or two. It also pairs well with all dairy produce and makes good herb butter or can be stirred into soft cheese for a scrumptious baked potato filling.

## SERVES 4

450 g (12 oz) haddock fillets
225 g (8 oz) potatoes, thinly sliced
50 g (2 oz) butter
225 g (8 oz) frozen peas
100 ml (3½ fl oz) white wine
1 onion, chopped
300 ml (10 fl oz) double cream
2 tomatoes, skinned, seeded and finely chopped
2 tablespoons chopped fresh parsley
1 tablespoon chopped fresh dill
2 tablespoons snipped fresh chives
Salt and freshly ground black pepper
Lemon wedges, to serve

# Five Favourite Ways with Salmon

think it's fair for me to say that salmon is my all-time favourite ingredient. I'm a bit partial to scallops and foie gras, but you don't often find them in supermarkets and with the recent great advances in fish farming, salmon has changed from being a luxury item to an affordable everyday favourite. I just love its versatility, unique flavour and texture, and it's healthy too! Make sure you buy Scottish farmed salmon – look for the tartan quality mark – as sadly not all farmed fish is as good as it should be.

The golden rule when cooking salmon is to veer towards keeping it underdone as there's nothing worse than overcooked salmon – it loses all its flavour and develops a texture similar to cotton wool.

**Choosing Fresh Fish** To make sure you're buying a spanking-fresh fish, look for these tell-tale signs:

bulging eyes – not hollow or dull
pink gills
slimy skin
firm texture
clean, non-fishy smell

If you want fillets of salmon, ask your fishmonger to cut the fillets for you or you can always buy ready-cut fillets from a supermarket.

**Salmon Tartare** The simplest way to enjoy salmon is to eat it raw and my favourite way to serve it is a tartare. You've got to start with a really fresh piece of fish so make sure you take note of the above points. Skin and bone the salmon then cut the flesh into 5 mm (¼ in) dice, stir in some finely chopped shallots, gherkins, Japanese-style pickled ginger and grated lemon rind and season well. Add a bit of fresh lemon juice, if you want to be fancy. Place a pastry cutter on a serving plate and pile in the tartare; lift off the ring and garnish with a cucumber salad and a dollop of crème fraîche.

**Seared Salmon Fillets** My absolute favourite way to eat salmon is when it's quickly seared in a hot pan – it's one of my signature dishes. To make it, you need to cut the salmon diagonally off the fillet in 5 mm (¼ in) thick slices. Heat a non-stick pan until it's very hot, then cook

the salmon on one side only for exactly 1 minute so it has a nice crisp top but is still moist on the bottom. I serve this with an avocado salsa, but you could try it on stir-fried greens, curried lentils, dressed salad leaves or on some pasta with a tomato or cream sauce. For a main course, 150–175 g (5–6 oz) of salmon fillets should be seared for 3–4 minutes on each side and for added texture and flavour, leave the skin on. Once the salmon is cooked, season it with sea salt (my favourite is Maldon), freshly ground white pepper, a squeeze of lemon juice and perhaps a splash of good olive oil. Who could ask for more?

**Roast Salmon** Roasting salmon is easy-peasy, and it's a particularly good way to cook wild salmon – which tends to have a slightly lower fat content than the farmed variety and is more prone to drying out during frying. You can roast fillets, steaks or even whole sides of salmon. I like to use flavourings such as citrus juice and a sprinkling of fresh herbs, particularly dill, chervil or basil. The method is very straightforward: to roast 150–175 g (5–6 oz) of fillets, heat the oven to 220°C/425°F/Gas 7, then heavily butter an ovenproof dish big enough to hold all the fillets without them touching. Arrange the fillets in the dish and squeeze over the juice, dot with a little extra butter and drizzle over a couple of tablespoons of water or white wine. Season with sea salt and white pepper and bang the dish into the oven for 7–8 minutes. Check if they're cooked by gently pressing the flesh – it should feel springy, not hard. Serve with the pan juices and creamy mashed potatoes.

**Poached Whole Salmon** If you have a whole salmon and a fish kettle (see below) then there's nothing nicer to serve on a summer's day than cold poached salmon with some mayonnaise or Hollandaise sauce. I love it with new-potato salad and some dressed watercress. To poach a whole salmon, fill a fish kettle two-thirds full with water, add a sliced lemon, a fresh bay leaf, a few peppercorns and parsley stalks and a tablespoon of sea salt. Bring to the boil, then lower in the salmon and cook over a high heat for 5–10 minutes. Turn off the heat, put on the lid and allow to stand overnight. The following day, remove the fish from the poaching liquid and then, using a knife and fork, peel back the skin and flake the flesh into big chunks of delicious, tender, moist salmon.

**Pastry-baked Salmon** Finally, salmon is great baked in pastry. The pastry seals in the flavour and gives you that lovely contrast between crisp pastry and tender salmon. I like to add extra flavourings – currants and preserved ginger work surprisingly well as do more traditional combinations such as asparagus, spinach and sorrel. The classic pastry choice is puff – rolled out very thinly and used to enclose 150 g (5 oz) fillets of salmon; carefully press to seal the edges, brush with a little beaten egg and sprinkle over some sea salt. Bake in an oven pre-heated to 220°C/425°F/Gas 7 for 7–8 minutes until well risen and golden brown. Filo pastry also works well – brush a sheet of pastry with melted butter and use to wrap the fillet; bake as for the puff pastry. Serve with a flavoursome sauce such as a *beurre blanc* with sorrel or a creamy watercress sauce or perhaps best of all, a classic Hollandaise.

# Pasta La Vista

Rigatoni (pasta tubes), onion, tomatoes, Double Gloucester, smoked haddock, spinach.

This creamy pasta made with gently poached smoked haddock and served with baked tomatoes makes a lovely mid-week supper.

**SERVES 4**

350 g (12 oz) rigatoni (pasta tubes)
4 tablespoons olive oil
1 onion, chopped
1 garlic clove, crushed
50 g (2 oz) fresh white breadcrumbs
Juice of ½ lemon
2 tablespoons chopped fresh parsley
10 small tomatoes
75 g (3 oz) Double Gloucester, grated
300 ml (10 fl oz) milk
225 g (8 oz) skinless, boneless smoked haddock
4 tablespoons white wine
150 ml (5 fl oz) double cream
2 tablespoons chopped fresh dill
225 g (8 oz) fresh spinach, stalks removed
Salt and freshly ground black pepper
Fresh dill sprigs, to garnish

Pre-heat the oven to 190°C/375°F/Gas 5. Cook the pasta in a large pan of boiling salted water for 10 minutes until tender.

Meanwhile, heat 2 tablespoons of the oil in a frying-pan and cook half the onion and the garlic for 5 minutes until softened. Stir in the breadcrumbs, lemon juice, parsley and salt and pepper to taste.

Cut the tops off 8 of the tomatoes then scoop out and discard the seeds. Spoon the breadcrumb mixture into the tomatoes and place in an ovenproof dish. Sprinkle over half the grated cheese and bake for 10 minutes until tender and golden.

Pour the milk into a shallow pan and heat gently. Add the fish and poach for 6–8 minutes until just cooked. Heat the remaining oil in a separate pan and cook the reserved onion for 5 minutes until softened. Chop the remaining 2 tomatoes and add to the onion pan with the wine, cream and dill. Season to taste and simmer gently for 5 minutes. Flake the haddock and stir into the sauce.

Place the spinach in a large pan, cover tightly and cook gently for 3–4 minutes until wilted.

Drain the pasta and place in a heatproof dish, pour over the cream sauce and sprinkle with the remaining cheese. Place under a pre-heated grill for 3–5 minutes until bubbling and golden. Arrange the spinach around the edge and garnish with the dill. Serve with the baked tomatoes.

Smoked haddock is a cold-smoked fish which means it is still raw and needs to be cooked, unlike hot-smoked fish such as the Arbroath Smokie (see page 65). It is available in its natural white state or is more often found dyed a bright yellow. Ideal for poaching, it can be substituted with other smoked white fish such as cod.

## ANTONY WORRALL THOMPSON
# Mussel Duet

Fresh mussels are marvellous. They're easy to cook, cheap, really good for you and they taste great!

 Live mussels, saffron strands.

Scrub the mussels, removing the gritty beards and discarding any that are damaged or do not close when tapped.

Place the prepared mussels in a large pan with the wine. Cover with a lid and cook over a high heat for 4–5 minutes until the mussels have opened. Remove the mussels with a large slotted spoon, discarding any that have not opened. Stir the saffron and cream into the liquor in the pan and simmer rapidly until reduced by half. Remove from the heat and add all but 12 of the mussels to the pan; cover to keep warm.

Stir together the butter, herbs, garlic and plenty of pepper. Snap the top shells off each of the reserved mussels and dot with the herby butter. Cook under a hot grill for 2–3 minutes until the butter is bubbling, then transfer to a serving dish. Turn the saffron mussels into a large bowl and serve.

Mussels are naturally very salty so you don't need to add salt to them during cooking. Make sure that you discard any cooked mussels that haven't opened.

### SERVES 2

900 g (2 lb) live mussels
300 ml (10 fl oz) dry white wine
Pinch of saffron strands
3 tablespoons double cream
75 g (3 oz) butter, softened
3 tablespoons chopped fresh herbs such as parsley, coriander, basil
2 garlic cloves, crushed
Freshly ground black pepper

Mussel Duet (page 73)

**Great Skate (page 76)**

# Great Skate

Skate wings, potato, fennel bulb, broccoli, yellow pepper, pickled capers.

I love cooking with skate; it has a wonderful texture and flavour and tastes fantastic served with this classic caper sauce, and accompanied by fennel rosti and a warm broccoli and yellow pepper salad.

### SERVES 2

100 ml (3½ fl oz) white wine
3 fresh thyme sprigs
1 fresh or dried bay leaf
6 black peppercorns
1 slice of lemon
1 tablespoon white wine vinegar
300 ml (10 fl oz) boiling water
2 x 175 g (6 oz) skate wings

### FOR THE ROSTI

1 large potato, coarsely grated
2 tablespoons olive oil
1 fennel bulb, quartered and thinly sliced
6 black peppercorns
Pinch of dried oregano

### FOR THE WARM SALAD

500 g (1 lb 2 oz) broccoli, cut into small florets
1 tablespoon olive oil
1 yellow pepper, seeded and chopped
Small handful fresh basil leaves

### FOR THE DRESSING

5 tablespoons white wine
1 tablespoon olive oil
1 teaspoon Dijon mustard
1 tablespoon white wine vinegar

### FOR THE SAUCE

50 g (2 oz) unsalted butter
2 tablespoons pickled capers, well rinsed
½ lemon
Salt and freshly ground black pepper

Place the wine, thyme, bay leaf, peppercorns, lemon, vinegar and boiling water in a large sauté pan, bring to the boil and simmer for 4 minutes.

Meanwhile, make the rosti. Dry the potato in a clean tea towel. Heat 1 tablespoon of the oil in a frying-pan and gently cook the fennel and peppercorns for 8 minutes until the fennel is softened. Transfer to a large bowl and stir in the potato, oregano and plenty of salt and pepper. Shape the mixture into round cakes about 2 cm (¾ in) thick. Heat the remaining oil in the same pan and cook the rosti for 3–4 minutes on each side until golden brown; keep warm in a low oven.

Add the skate to the pan of simmering water and cook for 10–12 minutes, turning once until just cooked.

Meanwhile, make the warm salad. Cook the broccoli in a pan of boiling salted water for 3 minutes. Drain well and cool under cold water. Heat the oil in a wok or large frying-pan and stir-fry the broccoli and pepper for 2–3 minutes until tender but still firm. Stir together the dressing ingredients and stir into the pan with the basil leaves. Cook for a further minute or so and season to taste.

To make the sauce, melt the butter in a small frying-pan, stir in the capers and a squeeze of lemon juice and cook over a high heat for 3–4 minutes until the butter is dark brown – take care not to let it burn.

To serve, place the rosti on two plates and arrange the skate wings on top. Pour round the sauce and serve with the warm salad.

Experiment by using different flavourings such as rosemary and lemon grass in the poaching liquid. And like any fish, skate should be very fresh – when past its best it has a slight ammonia smell and should be avoided.

**BRIAN TURNER**

# Super Stacks of Salmon

These mille-feuilles of salmon with new potatoes and spiced courgettes make a great Saturday or Sunday brunch dish for a warm summer's day.

Puff pastry, new potatoes, salmon steaks, onion, courgette.

Pre-heat the oven to 220°C/425°F/Gas 7. Roll out the pastry on a lightly floured surface to a thickness of 5 mm (¼ in). Using a 5 cm (2 in) pastry cutter, stamp out 6 circles of pastry. Transfer to a baking sheet, brush with egg yolk and bake for 10–15 minutes until well risen and golden brown.

Meanwhile, heat 2 tablespoons of the olive oil in a frying-pan and cook the sliced potatoes for 10–15 minutes, turning occasionally until golden brown.

Roll each steak up into a round and secure with cocktail sticks. Heat 1 tablespoon of oil in a separate frying-pan and cook the fish for 8 minutes, turning once until golden brown and just cooked through. Remove the cocktail sticks and cut each salmon steak in half horizontally.

Remove the pastry from the oven and lower the temperature to 200°C/400°F/Gas 6. Heat the remaining oil in a pan and cook the onion and courgette for 2 minutes. Stir in the cumin, cayenne, wholegrain mustard and a little seasoning and cook for a further 5 minutes until the vegetables are softened. Spoon the mixture into a buttered 10 cm (4 in) ramekin, pressing down well. Cook in the oven for 5 minutes.

Meanwhile, place the stock in a pan and bring to the boil. Continue to boil rapidly for 5 minutes until reduced by a third. Whisk in the butter, wine and Dijon mustard. Simmer gently for 3 minutes then stir in the chopped basil and salt and pepper to taste.

To serve, place two of the pastry discs on either side of a large plate and place a round of salmon on top. Continue to stack the remaining pastry and salmon rounds, finishing with a pastry round. Spoon the potatoes into the centre of the plate and turn out the timbale on top of the potatoes. Spoon over the Dijon sauce and garnish with the basil.

To reduce the liquor content of a sauce and concentrate the flavours, heat several empty pans until very hot and pour the boiling liquid from one pan to the other – as the liquid lands in each hot, empty pan, the evaporation process is dramatically speeded up.

**SERVES 2**

225 g (8 oz) puff pastry
1 egg yolk, lightly beaten
4 tablespoons olive oil
225 g (8 oz) new potatoes, thinly sliced
2 x 175 g (6 oz) boneless salmon steaks
1 small onion, finely chopped
1 courgette, diced
¼ teaspoon ground cumin
¼ teaspoon cayenne
1 teaspoon wholegrain mustard
300 ml (10 fl oz) fish or chicken stock
50 g (2 oz) unsalted butter
3 tablespoons white wine
1 teaspoon Dijon mustard
2 tablespoons chopped fresh basil
Salt and freshly ground black pepper
Fresh basil sprig, to garnish

# Crunchy Cod Steaks and Potato Cakes

Potatoes, streaky bacon, tomatoes, onion, green beans, cod steaks.

Cod is a lovely, firm-textured fish and is perfect for quick, simple cooking methods such as flash-frying.

**SERVES 2**

6 tablespoons olive oil
2 potatoes, thinly sliced
8 rashers streaky bacon, roughly chopped
2 tomatoes, sliced
2 garlic cloves, finely chopped
1 onion, finely chopped
150 ml (5 fl oz) red wine
½ chicken stock cube
½ teaspoon balsamic vinegar
150 g (5 oz) green beans, diagonally sliced
1 tomato, seeded and diced
2 x 150 g (5 oz) cod steaks
Salt and freshly ground black pepper

Pre-heat the oven to 220°C/425°F/Gas 7. Heat 3 tablespoons of the olive oil in a large ovenproof frying-pan. Place two 15 cm (6 in) cooking rings or pastry cutters in the pan and overlap a layer of potato slices in the bottom of the ring. Sprinkle with a little salt and pepper then scatter over half the chopped bacon. Arrange the sliced tomatoes over the bacon then sprinkle over half the chopped garlic. Finish with a final layer of potato slices and a little salt and pepper and continue to cook for a further 4 minutes until the underside is golden. Transfer the pan to the oven and cook for a further 15 minutes until the potato is tender.

Meanwhile, heat 1 tablespoon of oil in a pan and cook half the chopped onion, the remaining garlic and half of the remaining bacon over a high heat for 3–4 minutes until browned. Pour in the wine and bring to the boil then crumble in the stock cube and cook for 2–3 minutes. Add balsamic vinegar and salt and pepper to taste. Remove from the heat and cover to keep warm.

Heat 1 tablespoon of oil in a frying-pan and cook the remaining onion and bacon over a high heat for 3–4 minutes until browned. Stir in the beans and diced tomato and cook gently for 4–5 minutes, stirring occasionally until the beans are tender. Add salt and pepper to taste.

Meanwhile, heat the remaining 1 tablespoon of oil in a griddle pan and cook the cod for 3–4 minutes on each side until just cooked.

To serve, invert the potato cakes on to two plates. Arrange the cod steaks on top of the potato cakes then spoon over the beans. Pour round the sauce and serve.

Save time cooking the potato cakes by par-boiling the potatoes and frying the bacon before you layer them into the rings. Then simply cook in the pan for 3–4 minutes on each side until golden.

# En-Thai-Cing Spicy Curry

Rice, groundnut oil, baby sweetcorn, mangetout, green chilli, root ginger, spring onions, onion, button mushrooms, creamed coconut, dried lemon grass, Thai green curry paste, prawns.

No doubt about it, the taste of Thai is here to stay and everything in this recipe for Thai-style prawn curry is as close as your local supermarket – so why not give your tastebuds a real Thai-style thrill?

**SERVES 4**

½ teaspoon ground turmeric
225 g (8 oz) Thai Jasmine, basmati or long-grain rice
Groundnut oil, for frying
200 g (7 oz) baby sweetcorn, halved lengthways
200 g (7 oz) mangetout
½ fresh green chilli, seeded and thinly sliced
2.5 cm (1 in) piece of root ginger, grated
1 bunch of spring onions, thinly sliced
1 onion, finely chopped
150 g (5 fl oz) chicken or vegetable stock
Grated rind and juice of 1 lime
100 g (4 oz) button mushrooms, thinly sliced
75 g (3 oz) creamed coconut, coarsely grated
½ teaspoon dried lemon grass
1–2 tablespoons Thai green curry paste
225 g (8 oz) large cooked, peeled prawns
150 ml (5 fl oz) double cream
Salt and freshly ground black pepper
2 tablespoons chopped fresh coriander, to garnish

**For those with a peanut allergy, the groundnut oil in this recipe can be substituted with sunflower or vegetable oil.**

Stir the turmeric into a large pan of boiling water and cook the rice for 10–15 minutes, depending on the type used, until tender. Drain the rice well in a sieve, then sit the sieve over a pan of boiling water. Cover with a clean tea towel and leave for 2 minutes to help the grains fluff up.

Meanwhile, heat 1 tablespoon of the oil in a wok or large frying-pan and stir-fry the sweetcorn and mangetout over a very high heat for 1–2 minutes until lightly charred. Lower the heat and stir in the chilli, ginger, spring onions, onion, stock, lime juice, mushrooms, creamed coconut, lemon grass and curry paste and cook for 5 minutes, stirring occasionally until the vegetables are tender.

Stir in the prawns and cook for 2 minutes, then add the cream and cook for a further minute or two until the curry is piping hot. Add salt and pepper to taste.

To serve, spoon the rice on to plates and spoon over the curry. Garnish with coriander and lime rind.

Thai curry pastes are based on fresh flavourings such as garlic, coriander and lemon grass which are pounded together to make a wet paste. Traditionally Thai curry pastes are red or green, and the red, which is mainly used for beef curries, is coloured and flavoured with little dried red chillies. Authentic-tasting pastes are available from large supermarkets.

**PHIL VICKERY**

# Miso Mullet with Japanese Vegetables

This was the first time I'd ever used miso paste and I found it a little baffling but it seemed to work very well as a dressing for my red mullet.

Long-grain rice, red mullet, jar pickled yellow chillies, red peppers, Chinese leaf lettuce, miso paste.

Pre-heat the oven to 200°C/400°F/Gas 6. Heat 1 tablespoon of the olive oil in an ovenproof pan. Add the rice and dill, stirring to coat in the oil. Pour over the boiling water and season well with salt and pepper. Cook in the oven for 20 minutes until tender.

Meanwhile, diagonally score the fish three times on each side. Sprinkle over the balsamic vinegar, lime juice, 1 tablespoon of olive oil, the chives and a little salt and pepper.

To make the dressing, pour the oil into a bowl and whisk in the miso paste. Add half the lime juice, the balsamic vinegar, sugar, coriander and salt and pepper. In a separate bowl, stir together the double cream and remaining lime juice.

Heat 1 tablespoon of olive oil in a wok and stir-fry the chillies and peppers for 5 minutes until softened. Stir in the lettuce and cook for a further 3–4 minutes. Season with salt and pepper.

Brush the lime halves with the remaining oil and cook in a hot griddle pan, flesh-side down, for 2–3 minutes until lightly charred. Remove the limes from the pan and add the fish. Cook for 5–6 minutes until golden brown and just cooked. Remove the rice from the oven and spoon into two large, buttered ramekins, pressing down well.

To serve, turn out the rice on either side of a large plate. Spoon the stir-fried vegetables into the centre of the plate and drizzle over the dressing. Place the fish on top of the stir-fry and spoon over the lime cream.

 Miso is a thick paste made from fermented soya beans. It has a delicious, savoury flavour and is the base of the classic Japanese miso soup.

## SERVES 2

4 tablespoons olive oil
100 g (4 oz) long-grain rice
1 tablespoon chopped fresh dill
300 ml (10 fl oz) boiling water
1 red mullet, filleted
1 teaspoon balsamic vinegar
Juice of 1 lime
1 tablespoon chopped fresh chives
90 g jar of pickled yellow chillies, drained and roughly chopped
2 red peppers, seeded and sliced
1 Chinese leaf lettuce, shredded
1 lime, halved

### FOR THE DRESSING
3 tablespoons olive oil
1 tablespoon miso paste
Juice of 1 lime
1 tablespoon balsamic vinegar
1 tablespoon caster sugar
½ tablespoon chopped fresh coriander
2 tablespoons double cream
Salt and freshly ground black pepper

fish and shellfish

81

# POULTRY AND GAME

# First Class Chicken Parcels

Jerusalem artichokes, red onion, chicken thighs, button mushrooms, spring greens.

Chicken and Jerusalem artichokes are a perfect flavour marriage, so this tasty sauce beautifully complements the chicken.

### SERVES 2

225 g (8 oz) Jerusalem artichokes, peeled and thinly sliced
600 ml (1 pint) vegetable stock
1 red onion, chopped
1 teaspoon dried thyme
Pinch of grated nutmeg
50 g (2 oz) butter
4 boneless, skinless chicken thighs
100 g (4 oz) button mushrooms, quartered
Juice of ½ lemon
1 tablespoon chopped fresh parsley
225 g (8 oz) spring greens, stalks removed
6 tablespoons Greek yoghurt
Salt and freshly ground black pepper

Place the Jerusalem artichokes, stock, one quarter of the chopped red onion, ½ teaspoon of thyme and the nutmeg in a large pan. Bring to boil and simmer for 15 minutes until the artichokes are tender.

Meanwhile, melt half the butter in a large heavy-based frying-pan. Season the chicken well and add to the pan, skin-side down. Cook for 15 minutes, turning once, until crisp and golden brown.

Meanwhile, place the mushrooms, half the remaining onion, ½ teaspoon of thyme, half of the remaining butter, the lemon juice, parsley and 2 tablespoons of water in a small pan and cook gently for 10 minutes. Season to taste.

Add 4 of the largest spring green leaves to the pan of artichokes and cook for 2–3 minutes until tender. Remove from the pan and set aside to cool. Shred the remaining greens into 1 cm (½ in) ribbons. Remove the chicken from the frying-pan and set aside to rest. Melt the remaining butter in the chicken pan and stir-fry the shredded greens and remaining onion with 4 tablespoons of stock from the Jerusalem artichoke pan for 3–4 minutes until tender. Season to taste.

Drain the Jerusalem artichokes and place in a food processor with 2 tablespoons of the Greek yoghurt and blend until smooth. Place a chicken thigh in the centre of each cooked cabbage leaf and spoon 1 tablespoon of yoghurt on top of each. Neatly wrap the leaves around the chicken to make four parcels.

To serve, spoon the Jerusalem artichoke purée on to a large plate and arrange the chicken parcels on top. Drizzle round the mushroom sauce and serve the stir-fried greens in a separate bowl.

Treat Jerusalem artichokes like potatoes. They can be eaten in their skin but I prefer them peeled. They are excellent boiled, fried, roasted or mashed.

# Spicy Spinach-stuffed Chicken Legs

The turmeric-braised potatoes and cumin onions in this dish offer an Indian flavour and are delicious with the spinach-stuffed chicken.

Ground almonds, spinach, chicken legs, potatoes, onion.

Pre-heat the oven to 200°C/400°F/Gas 6.

To make the stuffing, in a large bowl beat together the eggs, cream, ground almonds and plenty of seasoning. Wash the spinach well and place in a large pan with a close-fitting lid. Cook gently for 3–4 minutes, shaking the pan occasionally until the spinach has wilted. Drain well then stir into the egg mixture.

Heat 2 tablespoons of oil in a large frying-pan and cook the chicken legs for 4–5 minutes, turning occasionally until well browned. Spoon the stuffing into the cavity left by the bone, then wrap each leg in buttered foil. Place the parcels in an ovenproof dish with 2 tablespoons of the stock and bake for 15–20 minutes until cooked through.

Meanwhile, heat the remaining oil in a separate frying-pan and cook the potatoes for 2–3 minutes. Pour over the wine and remaining stock and bring to the boil. Stir in the cardamom pods and simmer for 5–8 minutes until the potatoes are tender. Dice half the butter and whisk it into the potatoes with the turmeric. Stir in the coriander, then taste and adjust the seasoning if necessary.

Meanwhile, heat the remaining butter in a pan and cook the onion for 5 minutes until softened. Add the cumin and cook for a further 5 minutes until golden brown. Season to taste.

To serve, spoon the onion on to a plate and arrange the stuffed chicken legs on top. Spoon round the turmeric potatoes and serve immediately.

Breast of chicken can be used for this dish but it is more expensive and, in my view, not as tasty as good old legs.

## SERVES 2

2 eggs
150 ml (5 fl oz) double cream
75 g (3 oz) ground almonds
225 g (8 oz) fresh spinach, stalks removed
3 tablespoons sunflower oil
2 chicken legs, thigh bone removed
150 ml (5 fl oz) chicken stock
2 potatoes, diced
150 ml (5 fl oz) white wine
5 cardamom pods, cracked
50 g (2 oz) butter
2 teaspoons ground turmeric
1 teaspoon chopped fresh coriander
1 onion, finely chopped
1 teaspoon ground cumin
Salt and freshly ground black pepper

AINSLEY HARRIOTT'S

# Five Favourite Ways with Chicken

**W**ith our busy lifestyles, most of us want a meal that's quick to cook but also nutritious, tasty and easy to present beautifully. That's why I've chosen chicken. It's the most versatile meat and can be bought in a wide range of cuts and joints, with or without skin, indeed even stuffed, and we all like a good stuffing! Don't be quick to discard the skin before cooking as it protects the flesh, keeping the meat nice and moist for eating.

Choosing a Bird: If you're feeling posh or just fancy a change, try corn-fed chicken. It has a slightly yellow tinge and tastes a little like pheasant. The free-range variety has a far superior flavour to that of your average chicken and isn't that much more expensive – remember, eat well, keep well! Poussin is small spring chicken which is really easy to cook, especially on the barbecue, and if you're a bone sucker, you'll love them!

Cooking Chicken Safely: Always use separate utensils for raw and cooked chicken. Clean chopping boards and work surfaces thoroughly after use, as food-poisoning bacteria can easily be transferred to hands and other foods. To make sure your chicken is thoroughly cooked, simply pierce the thickest part of the meat and apply a little pressure to release the juices which should show no signs of pinkness.

So now you know the rules, let's get cooking!

**Baked Lemon Splash Spatchcock Chicken** For those who like it spicy, sprinkle a pinch of dried chillies over the chicken before roasting. Serves two as a main course.

Using a sturdy pair of kitchen scissors, cut down the backbone of a small, whole chicken, then flatten it out with the heel of the hand. Thread two long metal skewers diagonally through the bird to hold it flat. Place in a roasting tin.

In a small bowl, mix some olive oil, 2 cloves of crushed garlic, a handful of chopped, fresh parsley, the grated rind of a lemon and salt and freshly ground black pepper. Drizzle the mixture over the bird and leave to marinate for at least 2 hours, turning occasionally and basting with the marinade. Squeeze over the lemon juice and roast in an oven pre-heated to 200°C/400°F/Gas 6 for an hour until golden brown and cooked through. Simply great with a crunchy salad and garlic bread.

**Chicken Phuket with Roasted Spiced Vegetables and Glass Noodles** My wife constantly surprises me by inviting friends to dinner at short notice and it was on one of those occasions that this recipe was born.

Season boneless chicken breasts or thighs with Chinese five-spice powder, then fry in a hot pan with a little sunflower oil and a finely chopped onion, turning until well browned. Pour in a couple of cartons of coconut cream, stir in 2 teaspoons of Thai red curry paste and bring to the boil. Meanwhile, roast some diced carrots, celery, courgettes, aubergine and halved cherry tomatoes in a very hot oven for 5 minutes, then stir into the chicken mixture with 2 tablespoons of crunchy peanut butter. Add salt and pepper and cook for 15 minutes. Cook some rice noodles according to the packet instructions, drain well and toss with a little sesame oil. Place the noodles on a serving platter and spoon over the chicken. Sprinkle with toasted sesame seeds and serve.

**Crisp-crumb Cheesy Chicken** A simple idea that's always pleasing, and one which the kids love making and eating.

Mix together some fresh white breadcrumbs, 2 tablespoons of freshly grated Parmesan and plenty of salt and pepper. Dip 4 boneless, skinless chicken breasts into seasoned flour, then beaten egg and finally, roll them in the cheesy breadcrumb mixture. Heat 2 tablespoons of olive oil in a frying-pan and cook the chicken for 8 minutes on each side until the coating is golden brown and the chicken is cooked through. Serve with salad or make into a sandwich with crusty bread and a dollop of mayonnaise. Serves four.

**Tandoori Chicken** This classic Punjab speciality is normally eaten at dawn in your favourite Indian restaurant – now you can make it at home and still produce stunning results. This quantity serves four.

In a large bowl mix together: 150 g (5 oz) natural yoghurt, 2 tablespoons gram flour, 4 crushed garlic cloves, 1 tablespoon grated root ginger, 1 tablespoon finely chopped green chilli, a pinch of dried red chilli flakes, ½ teaspoon ground cumin, 1 teaspoon ground turmeric, a pinch of freshly grated nutmeg, a handful of chopped fresh mint and coriander, the juice of 1 lemon and plenty of salt and pepper. Add 4 chicken quarters and leave to marinate for at least 4 hours, turning occasionally and basting with the marinade. Cook in an oven pre-heated to 180°C/350°F/Gas 4 for 30–40 minutes until cooked through. Place under a hot grill for 1–2 minutes until the chicken skin is slightly charred. Serve with lemon wedges, mango chutney and naan bread.

**Sizzling Chicken Fajitas** Bring a touch of Mexico into your kitchen with this simple but extremely tasty meal for two. Most supermarkets now sell flour tortillas.

Heat a tablespoon of sunflower oil in a wok and stir-fry 2 sliced chicken breasts, 1 sliced red pepper and 1 sliced red onion for 2 minutes. Sprinkle over a pinch of dried oregano and salt and pepper and stir-fry for another few minutes. Squeeze over the juice of 1 lime and sprinkle with a tablespoon of chopped fresh coriander. Scatter some shredded lettuce on 4 flour tortillas and spoon the chicken mixture on top. Drizzle a spoonful of soured cream over each and roll up. Wash down with some ice-cold lager with a splash of fresh lime.

**ANTHONY TOBIN**

# Chicken and Watercress Pasta

Chicken breasts, shallots, watercress, fresh tagliolini tricolore (multi-coloured pasta ribbons), tomatoes.

I'm a real pasta fan and this dish is packed with flavour and texture but be warned, my portions are pretty generous.

### SERVES 2

2 x 75 g (3 oz) boneless, skinless chicken breasts, sliced into 1 cm (½ in) wide strips
8 tablespoons olive oil
3 tablespoons chopped, mixed fresh herbs, e.g. parsley, basil, coriander and chives
2 shallots, finely chopped
2 tablespoons balsamic vinegar
75 g (3 oz) watercress
1 small garlic clove, crushed
Juice of ½ lemon
1 teaspoon ground turmeric
250 g (9 oz) fresh tagliolini tricolore (multi-coloured pasta ribbons)
Salt and freshly ground black pepper

### TO GARNISH

2 tomatoes, skinned, seeded and finely diced
1 tablespoon snipped fresh chives

Place the chicken strips in a large bowl with 2 tablespoons of the olive oil, the chopped herbs and plenty of salt and pepper and toss well together. Heat a large non-stick frying-pan and cook the chicken strips for 3–4 minutes, then add the shallots and balsamic vinegar and continue to cook for a further 2–3 minutes until the chicken is cooked through and well browned and the shallots are tender. Add salt and pepper to taste.

Blanch the watercress in a large pan of boiling salted water for 30 seconds, then drain well. Place in a food processor with 3 tablespoons of olive oil and blend for 1 minute. Add the garlic and lemon juice and whizz again until smooth. Season to taste.

Place 2 tablespoons of the olive oil in a small pan and stir in the ground turmeric. Heat very gently for 2–3 minutes then strain the oil through a piece of muslin or a clean cloth to remove the turmeric.

Cook the pasta in a large pan of boiling salted water for 3–4 minutes until tender. Drain well and toss with the remaining tablespoon of olive oil.

To serve, place the pasta in two large serving bowls and spoon the chicken mixture on top. Pour round the watercress sauce and drizzle over the turmeric oil. Garnish with the diced tomatoes and snipped chives.

Fresh pasta is readily available in supermarket chill cabinets in an ever-growing range of shapes and sizes. Many of the varieties have wonderful fillings and all can be cooked in just a few minutes. Of course this recipe can be cooked very successfully with dried pasta.

**RICHARD CAWLEY**

# Crispy Chicken Tropicana

A superb, exotic-flavoured dish adding real interest to ordinary supermarket chicken pieces. It's worth making a double quantity of the pineapple salsa as any leftovers will add zest to sandwiches, sausages and cold-cuts. *Illustrated on page 82.*

 Chicken thighs, easy-cook rice, spring onions, red chilli, green pepper, tinned pineapple chunks in natural juice.

Remove the skin from the chicken and discard. Cut the flesh away from the bone; reserve the bones and cut the flesh into 1 cm (½ in) wide strips and set aside.

Place the water in large pan. Add the stock cube, chicken bones and rice and bring to the boil. Stir in the orange rind and half of the orange juice, spring onions, chilli and green pepper. Cook for 10 minutes or according to packet instructions, until tender. Add salt and pepper to taste.

To make the salsa, stir together the pineapple and lime juice with the remaining spring onions, chilli, green pepper and orange juice. Season with salt and pepper, then transfer to a serving bowl.

In a small bowl, mix together the cornflour and mixed spice. Coat the chicken strips in the spiced flour, shaking off any excess. Deep-fry in batches for 4–5 minutes until cooked through and golden brown. Drain on kitchen paper.

Deep-fry the thyme sprigs and basil leaves for 30 seconds. Drain on kitchen paper.

Remove the chicken bones from the rice and discard. To serve, spoon the rice on to plates and arrange the fried chicken on top. Garnish with the deep-fried herbs and serve with the salsa.

 It is important to use a small, very sharp, pointed knife when boning chicken and always work with the blade of the knife angled away from you to prevent accidents.

SERVES 2

4 chicken thighs
400 ml (14 fl oz) water
1 chicken stock cube
225 g (8 oz) easy-cook rice
Grated rind and juice of 1 orange
1 bunch of spring onions, finely chopped
1 red chilli, seeded and finely chopped
1 green pepper, seeded and chopped
220 g tin of pineapple chunks in natural juice, drained and roughly chopped
Juice of 1 lime
2 tablespoons cornflour
1 teaspoon ground mixed spice
Vegetable oil, for deep-frying
2 fresh thyme sprigs
2 fresh basil leaves
Salt and freshly ground black pepper

## ANTONY WORRALL THOMPSON
# Cause a Stir-fry

Flavours of ginger, lemon grass, soy and coriander are all the rage, and are a wonderful combination for this oriental-style dish of stir-fried chicken and prawns with noodles.

Ginger purée, dried lemon grass, courgette, red pepper, spring onions, chicken breasts, rice noodles, tiger prawns, fish sauce.

Pound the garlic in a pestle and mortar to form a paste. Stir in the ginger purée and lemon grass.

Heat 3 tablespoons of the olive oil in a wok or large frying-pan and stir-fry the courgette, red pepper and spring onions for 2 minutes. Add the chicken strips and cook for 4–5 minutes until cooked through. Remove from the heat and set aside.

To make the omelettes, beat the eggs with a little seasoning. Melt half the butter in a large, separate frying-pan and pour in half the beaten eggs. Swirl around the pan and cook for 2–3 minutes on each side. Slide the omelette out of the pan and repeat with the remaining butter and beaten egg. Roll up both omelettes and cut into 5 mm (¼ in) thick slices.

Place the rice noodles in a large heatproof bowl and pour over the boiling water. Set aside for 4–5 minutes.

Heat the sunflower oil in the pan used for the omelettes and cook the prawns for 30 seconds until pink. Add 2 teaspoons of fish sauce and cook for a further 20 seconds or so until just cooked. Remove from the heat.

Heat the remaining tablespoon of olive oil in a clean wok and stir-fry the garlic paste mixture for 1 minute. Drain the noodles and add to the wok with the remaining fish sauce and the soy sauce. Stir in the prawns, chicken and vegetables, the omelette slices, chopped coriander and chives and stir-fry for 1–2 minutes until piping hot. Transfer to a large bowl and garnish with the coriander leaves.

Stir-frying is one of the fastest ways of cooking vegetables. Cooked this way, they also retain their 'crunch', colour and nutritional content.

## SERVES 4

4 garlic cloves
2 teaspoons ginger purée
1 teaspoon dried lemon grass
4 tablespoons olive oil
1 courgette, thinly sliced
1 red pepper, seeded and chopped
5 spring onions, sliced diagonally
100 g (4 oz) chicken breasts,
cut into 1 cm (½ in) strips
3 eggs
25 g (1 oz) butter
200 g (7 oz) rice noodles
600 ml (1 pint) boiling water
1 tablespoon sunflower oil
250 g (9 oz) raw, peeled tiger prawns
4 teaspoons fish sauce
1 tablespoon soy sauce
2 tablespoons chopped fresh coriander
and chives
Salt and freshly ground black pepper
Fresh coriander leaves, to garnish

# Rich and Creamy Chicken Ravioli

Chicken breasts, onion, carrots, courgettes.

Don't be scared to try making your own fresh pasta – once you've practised it a few times, you'll soon get to know how the dough should feel and believe me, the results are well worth the effort.

### SERVES 4 AS A STARTER

225 g (8 oz) boneless, skinless chicken breasts
2 eggs and 1 egg yolk
300 ml (½ pt )cream
Small handful of fresh basil
165 g (5½ oz) plain flour
50 g (2 oz) unsalted butter
1 onion, chopped
5 tablespoons white wine
2 tablespoons snipped fresh chives
2 carrots, cut into long, fine matchsticks
Juice of ½ orange
2 courgettes
Juice of ½ lemon
Salt and freshly ground black pepper
Snipped fresh chives, to garnish

Home-made pasta dough freezes very well, so it can be made in advance. The ravioli themselves can be made up to 12 hours ahead. Cook them as instructed in the recipe, then cool in iced water, lay them on a tray, cover with a clean towel then wrap the whole tray in plastic film and chill until ready to serve. To re-heat, simply plunge the ravioli into a pan of boiling salted water for 90 seconds.

Place the chicken breasts, 1 egg, 4 tablespoons of the cream, the basil and plenty of salt and pepper in a food processor and whizz until smooth.

Place the flour, remaining egg and the egg yolk in a clean food processor and whizz until the mixture comes together to form a firm dough. Tip the dough out on to a floured surface and knead for several minutes until smooth.

Roll the dough through the widest setting of a pasta machine about 5–6 times, folding the dough in half between each roll. When the dough is smooth and elastic, continue to pass through the machine, using a thinner setting each time to give a long, thin sheet of pasta. Using a 7.5 cm (3 in) pastry cutter, stamp out 16 circles of pasta.

Place a heaped teaspoon of the chicken mixture in the centre of 8 of the circles; dampen the edges with a little water. Use the remaining rounds to cover the filling. Press the edges together to seal but try not to trap any air inside the ravioli.

Cook the ravioli in a large pan of simmering salted water for 6–8 minutes until tender. Drain well.

Meanwhile, melt half the butter in a small pan. Cook the onion for 3 minutes until softened, then pour in the wine, the remaining cream, and salt and pepper to taste. Cook gently for 5 minutes, then stir in the snipped chives.

Meanwhile, place the carrots in a separate pan with half the remaining butter, the orange juice and seasoning. Cook for 3–4 minutes until tender. Drain well.

Using a swivel-style vegetable peeler, thinly slice the courgettes lengthways into ribbons. Heat the remaining 15 g (½ oz) butter in a large frying-pan and add the courgette ribbons and the lemon juice. Cook for 2–3 minutes until just tender, then season to taste.

To serve, place a pile of courgettes in the centre of a plate and place a ravioli on top. Pour over some of the cream sauce, top with the carrot, and sprinkle with the chives.

**AINSLEY HARRIOTT**

# Cheesy Chicken Parcels

The Greeks have been stuffing vine leaves for years with a whole variety of ingredients, but I'm sure they'd be equally impressed with my filling of chicken and feta cheese. Served with a tomato sauce, this dish really captures the taste of the Mediterranean and looks stunning, too!

Long-grain rice, chicken breast, feta cheese, preserved vine leaves, spring onions, tomatoes, pitted black olives.

Cook the rice in boiling salted water for 15–20 minutes until tender. Drain well and spoon into two buttered ramekins or teacups, patting down well.

Meanwhile, make the vine leaf parcels. Place a piece of chicken and 2 cubes of feta on each vine leaf, then roll up, tucking in the ends to make 9 neat parcels. Season with salt and pepper, then thread the parcels on to 3 skewers. Heat 1 tablespoon of the olive oil in a frying-pan and cook the parcels for 5 minutes, turning frequently. Drizzle over the remaining oil, then remove from the pan and cook under a pre-heated grill for 15–20 minutes, turning occasionally, until the chicken is cooked.

To make the sauce, heat the olive oil in a pan and cook the spring onions and garlic for 1 minute. Stir in the tomatoes and wine, bring to the boil then cover and simmer for 10–12 minutes until the sauce has reduced to a fairly thick consistency. Add salt and pepper to taste.

To serve, turn the rice out on to a plate. Spoon the sauce to one side of the plate and arrange the vine leaf parcels on top of the sauce. Garnish with the olive slices.

Vine leaves are traditionally used in Greek cookery. If you are lucky enough to get hold of fresh leaves, blanch them for a few minutes in boiling water before use. The preserved variety are readily available in specialist stores and large supermarkets but they should be soaked for about half an hour in hot water to help remove the salt they are preserved in.

## SERVES 2

150 g (5 oz) long-grain rice
200 g (7 oz) skinless, boneless chicken breast, cut into 9 even-sized strips
175 g (6 oz) feta cheese, cut into 18 cubes
9 preserved vine leaves, drained
2 tablespoons olive oil

## FOR THE SAUCE

3 tablespoons olive oil
2 spring onions, thinly sliced
2 garlic cloves, finely chopped
6 tomatoes, skinned, seeded and thinly sliced
3 tablespoons white wine
Salt and freshly ground black pepper

6 stoned black olives, sliced, to garnish

Cheesy Chicken Parcels (page 93)

Lovely Chicken Livers with Lashings of Mash (page 96)

# Lovely Chicken Livers with Lashings of Mash

Floury potatoes, red onion, oyster mushrooms, Cheddar or Mozzarella, black treacle, chicken livers, Savoy cabbage, baby salad leaves.

Chicken livers are great value for money, but take care not to overcook them. The soft, creamy texture of the livers, mashed potato and onion gravy is perfectly complemented by the crunchy cabbage in this tasty dish.

## SERVES 2

500 g (1 lb 2 oz) floury potatoes, cut into 2.5 cm (1 in) cubes
5 tablespoons olive oil
1 red onion, thinly sliced
150 g (5 oz) oyster mushrooms
100 g (4 oz) Cheddar or Mozzarella, diced
Few basil leaves, roughly torn
Grated rind and juice of 1 lemon
150 ml (5 fl oz) red wine
1 tablespoon black treacle
600 ml (1 pint) hot chicken stock
200 g (7 oz) unsalted butter
400 g (14 oz) chicken livers, trimmed
½ Savoy cabbage, roughly chopped
2 tablespoons snipped fresh chives
2 tablespoons chopped fresh chervil
1 garlic clove, finely chopped
100 g bag baby salad leaves
Salt and freshly ground black pepper
Snipped fresh chives, to garnish

If you want to make lovely, creamy mash, it is important to start with a good, floury potato such as King Edward, Desirée or Maris Piper. Peel and cut them into 2.5 cm (1 in) cubes, then cook slowly in boiling, salted water – don't use a rolling boil as this makes them soggy and liable to break up in the pan. Drain the cooked potatoes well, then dry out in a the pan or a hot oven for 5–10 minutes. Use a masher, potato ricer or mouli to remove all the lumps, then with a wooden spoon beat in some olive oil or butter until light and fluffy. Season with plenty of salt and pepper.

Pre-heat the oven to 220°C/425°F/Gas 7. Cook the potatoes in large pan of boiling salted water for 20 minutes, until tender.

Meanwhile, heat 1 tablespoon of the olive oil in a large frying-pan and gently cook the red onion for 5 minutes, until softened.

Place the mushrooms in an oiled ovenproof dish and scatter over the cheese. Drizzle over 2 tablespoons of the olive oil, the basil and half of the lemon rind and juice. Season well and place in the oven for 5–7 minutes until the mushrooms are tender and the cheese is melted and bubbling.

Place the red wine and treacle in a separate pan, bring to the boil, then simmer rapidly until reduced by half. Add 2 tablespoons of the stock to the onion pan and then pour the remaining stock into the wine pan. Continue to simmer the wine liquid until reduced by half, then gradually whisk in 50 g (2 oz) of the butter, stir in the red onions and season to taste.

Heat 1 tablespoon of olive oil in a separate, heavy-based frying-pan and cook the livers for 2 minutes on each side until well browned but still

pink in the centre. Add the remaining lemon juice and salt and pepper to taste, and cook for a further 2–3 minutes. Remove from the pan and cover with foil, to keep warm.

Add the cabbage to the hot pan used for the livers and cook for 5 minutes, stirring frequently until tender and beginning to brown on the edges; season well.

Drain the potatoes and mash well with the remaining 1 tablespoon of olive oil, 25 g (1 oz) of butter and the chopped herbs; season to taste.

To make the warm dressing, melt the remaining 100 g (4 oz) of butter in a small pan and stir in the garlic and remaining lemon rind; season to taste.

To serve, spoon the mash into the centre of a large plate and pile the cabbage on top. Arrange the livers on the cabbage. Pour round the wine sauce and garnish with chives. Place the salad leaves on a separate serving plate and spoon on the cheesy mushrooms. Drizzle over the butter dressing and serve immediately.

ROSS BURDEN

# Chicken on a Stick with Saffron Risotto

Saffron is my favourite spice but it needs to be handled carefully and kept away from light, which destroys its flavour. English saffron was exported to Turkey in the 14th and 15th centuries.

Savoy cabbage, onion, risotto rice, saffron strands, chicken breasts, button mushrooms, red pepper.

Remove any damaged outer leaves from the cabbage. Gently fold back the remaining outer leaves and cut out the middle so you are left with a cabbage 'basket'. Place the cabbage basket in a pan quarter-filled with boiling salted water and cook for 10 minutes until tender. Drain well and cool under cold water.

Meanwhile, melt the butter in a separate pan, add the onion and cook gently for 3–4 minutes until softened.

Bring 1.2 litres (2 pints) of water to the boil in a separate pan and add the stock cubes and 150 ml (5 fl oz) wine; keep this stock just simmering.

Add the rice to the softened onion and stir to coat in the butter. Pour in 2 ladles of the hot stock, add the saffron and stir gently. Leave to simmer gently and when the stock has been absorbed, add a further 2 ladles of hot stock, stir and leave to simmer again. Continue this process until the rice is tender – it takes about 20 minutes.

Slice the chicken into 2 cm (¾ in) pieces and place in a bowl with 3 tablespoons of the olive oil and the lemon juice. Stir to coat and set aside for 5 minutes, to marinate.

Thread the chicken, mushrooms and pepper on to 4 skewers and season well. Cook in a hot griddle pan or large frying-pan for 8 minutes, turning occasionally until golden brown. Drizzle over the remaining wine and cook for a further 2 minutes until the chicken is cooked through.

Shred the central, uncooked cabbage leaves. Heat the remaining olive oil in a wok or large frying-pan set over a high heat and stir-fry the cabbage for 2–3 minutes until tender. Season to taste.

In a small bowl, mix together orange rind, half the chopped parsley and the crushed garlic.

To serve, place the cabbage basket in a deep serving bowl and fill the base with shredded cabbage. Fill with the risotto and place the kebabs on top. Sprinkle over the orange rind mixture and top with the remaining parsley.

For a cheap alternative to saffron, substitute turmeric, which gives the same colour but without the glorious flavour of the original.

## SERVES 4

1 Savoy cabbage
25 g (1 oz) butter
1 onion, finely chopped
1.2 litres (2 pints) water
2 chicken stock cubes
250 ml (9 fl oz) white wine
225 g (8 oz) risotto rice
10–15 saffron strands
2 skinless, boneless chicken breasts
5 tablespoons olive oil
Juice of 1 lemon
150 g (5 oz) button mushrooms
1 large red pepper, seeded and cut into bite-sized pieces
Finely grated rind of 1 orange
2 tablespoons chopped fresh parsley
3 garlic cloves, crushed
Salt and freshly ground black pepper

# Chicken and Spicy Sausage Sensation

Talk about 'flavour explosion'! – my heart leapt with excitement when the ingredients popped out of the bag for this programme. It's one of my favourite dishes from the show.

Fusilli tricolore (multi-coloured pasta spirals), chicken breast, onion, tinned cherry tomatoes, chorizo, Little Gem lettuces, Parmesan or Pecorino.

Place the egg in pan of boiling water and cook for 10 minutes. Drain well and cool under cold water.

Meanwhile, cook the pasta in a large pan of boiling salted water for 12–15 minutes, until tender. Drain well and toss with 1 tablespoon of the olive oil; keep warm.

Heat the butter and 1 tablespoon of the sunflower oil in a wok and stir-fry the chicken pieces for 4–5 minutes until well browned. Remove with a slotted spoon and set aside.

Add the onion to the pan and cook for 1 minute. Stir in the wine, tomatoes and Worcestershire sauce and simmer rapidly until the liquid has reduced by half. Stir in 3 tablespoons of the cream, the Tabasco sauce, and salt and pepper to taste.

Heat 1 tablespoon of oil in two separate frying-pans. Cook the bread dice in one pan for 3–4 minutes, shaking the pan until crisp and golden brown. In the second pan, cook the chorizo for 2–3 minutes until the edges begin to brown.

Stir the chicken and chorizo into the tomato sauce with the remaining 2 tablespoons of cream.

To make the salad dressing, whisk together the remaining olive oil, the wine vinegar and mustard and season to taste.

To serve, separate the lettuce leaves and place on a plate. Coarsely grate over the hard-boiled egg and drizzle over the dressing; scatter with the croûtons. Turn the pasta into a large serving bowl and pour over the chicken and chorizo sauce. Sprinkle with Parmesan and garnish with the chives.

Chorizo is one of the great sausages from Spain. Highly seasoned, roughly ground pork is flavoured with garlic, chilli and other spices before being cured. It is also used in Mexican cooking when the skin is removed and the sausage crumbled into casseroles, soups and stews. Said by many to be good cooked on a barbecue, and I've even had it as a garnish to a baked fish dish and found it deliciously different!

## SERVES 2

1 egg
250 g (9 oz) fusilli tricolore (multi-coloured pasta spirals)
4 tablespoons olive oil
25 g (1 oz) butter
3 tablespoons sunflower oil
100 g (4 oz) boneless, skinless chicken breast, cut into bite-sized pieces
1 onion, finely chopped
100 ml (4 fl oz) white wine
395 g tin of cherry tomatoes
½ teaspoon Worcestershire sauce
5 tablespoons double cream
Few drops of Tabasco sauce
1 slice white bread, crusts removed, diced
50 g (2 oz) piece chorizo, diced
1 tablespoon white wine vinegar
½ teaspoon Dijon mustard
2 Little Gem lettuce
2 tablespoons freshly grated Parmesan or Pecorino
Salt and freshly ground black pepper
Snipped fresh chives, to garnish

LESLEY WATERS

# Fantastic Paella and Peppers

Onion, fennel bulb, chicken breasts, long-grain rice, red pepper, tinned chopped tomatoes.

This may not be an authentic Spanish-style paella but nonetheless, the results are very tasty.

**SERVES 4**

2 tablespoons olive oil
1 onion, chopped
1 fennel bulb, chopped
2 garlic cloves, crushed
450 g (1 lb) boneless, skinless chicken breasts, cut into 1 cm (½ in) dice
350 g (12 oz) long-grain rice
1 teaspoon ground turmeric
100 ml (3½ fl oz) white wine
600 ml (1 pint) vegetable or chicken stock
Grated rind and juice of 1 lime
1 tablespoon chopped fresh parsley

**FOR THE PEPPERS**

1 red pepper, halved and seeded
2 tablespoons olive oil
400 g tin of chopped tomatoes

**FOR THE DRESSING**

3 tablespoons olive oil
2 tablespoons white wine vinegar
2 tablespoons chopped fresh parsley
1 teaspoon English mustard
2 teaspoons water
Salt and freshly ground black pepper

Pre-heat the oven to 200°C/400°F/Gas 6. Heat the oil in a pan and cook the onion, three-quarters of the fennel, the garlic and half the chicken for 4 minutes. Stir in the rice, turmeric, wine, stock and seasoning; bring to the boil, cover and simmer for 10–15 minutes until the liquid has been absorbed and the rice is tender. Check regularly, adding more stock if the rice becomes too dry.

Meanwhile, place the pepper halves, cut-side down on a baking sheet and brush with a tablespoon of the olive oil. Roast for 10 minutes.

Heat the remaining tablespoon of oil in a separate pan and cook the reserved fennel and chicken for 4 minutes. Add the tomatoes and simmer for 5 minutes; season to taste.

Meanwhile, make the dressing. Whisk together the oil, vinegar, parsley, mustard and water. Season to taste and pour over the peppers.

To serve, spoon the chicken and tomato mixture into the roasted peppers and place on four plates. Stir the lime rind and juice, and the parsley into the paella and divide between the plates.

The turmeric adds a lovely colour to the rice but for a real touch of luxury, soak a pinch of saffron strands in some warm water and use in its place.

**AINSLEY HARRIOTT**

# Lemon Chicken with Fried Thyme Tatties

Now ... if you're one of those people who thicken their sauces with flour, cornflour, arrowroot or lots of reduced cream, here's a great alternative that promises you a rich, creamy sauce that tastes wonderful and is incredibly easy to make.

 Chicken, fresh tarragon, potatoes.

Season the chicken pieces with salt and pepper. Heat the oil in a large pan and cook the chicken for 5 minutes, turning frequently until well browned. Drain off any excess fat and stir in the tarragon and white wine; simmer rapidly until the liquid is reduced by half. Pour in the stock and cook for a further 2–3 minutes until the chicken is cooked through.

Whisk together the lemon juice and egg yolks and add to the chicken, stirring continuously. Cook for 3–4 minutes, stirring to produce a smooth, thickened sauce. Season with salt and pepper.

Meanwhile, cook the potatoes in a large pan of boiling salted water for 15 minutes. Drain well.

Heat the olive oil and butter in a large frying-pan and add the potatoes, thyme and a little salt and pepper. Cook for 5 minutes until tender and golden brown.

To serve, pile the sautéed potatoes on to a plate and spoon over the saucy lemon chicken.

We don't often think of egg yolks as a thickening agent, but when you realise that mayonnaise, Hollandaise, even fresh custard sauce are made using egg yolks, it all makes perfect sense. One word of warning though, once you've added the egg yolks to the warm sauce, do not bring it back to the boil or the sauce will separate and you'll end up with tiny bits of scrambled egg floating around ...

**SERVES 2**

275 g (10 oz) boneless chicken, cut into bite-sized pieces
1 tablespoon vegetable oil
2 tablespoons chopped fresh tarragon
150 ml (5 fl oz) white wine
250 ml (8 fl oz) hot chicken stock
Juice of 1 lemon
3 egg yolks
2 large, unpeeled potatoes, diced
1 tablespoon olive oil
25 g (1 oz) butter
2 fresh thyme sprigs
Salt and freshly ground black pepper

# Guide to Successful Dinner Parties

To many people, even those who cook well, the thought of preparing a complete meal for a substantial number of guests is a daunting task. However, potential culinary disasters can easily be avoided with a little careful preparation. So how do you prepare for that special dinner party and at the same time transform the kitchen from a 'workhouse' into a relaxed environment in which you can produce stunning dishes that are guaranteed to titillate and tantalize the palate? Good planning is the key to success and by following these golden rules you will feel relaxed and happy when your guests arrive.

The first and most important consideration when planning your menu is to discover as much about your guests as possible. For example, you might want to discover their likes and dislikes, whether they have any food allergies (or fetishes) and so forth. If it proves impossible to obtain this information then you need to adopt the 'belt and braces' approach, in other words, take precautions. Select dishes that can be adapted to suit vegetarians and have alternatives available for those who may be gluten or dairy free. In addition, a successful menu needs to be balanced. Plan a light course before and after a heavy course. Similarly, consider the colours of the ingredients for each course in order to ensure that the combination of colours in the dishes look attractive when they are presented. Not only do the dishes need to look good, they also need to stimulate the palate, so include a range of tastes and textures that will excite the taste buds.

The second golden rule is to prepare as much in advance as possible. It is a huge mistake to construct a menu that places demands on your time during the meal. You deserve to enjoy the occasion as much as your guests and you can only do this if you are relaxed and in control. So choose dishes that can be prepared fully or at least partly in advance and then you will have more time to garnish them just before they are served.

The third golden rule is to use recipes that you know will work. The evening of the dinner party is not the time to try out new recipes. I always try my new dinner-party dishes on the family first.

Finally, whenever possible, use fresh, seasonal ingredients, as these tend to have more taste and are often cheaper because they are in abundance. Nevertheless, it is still fun to incorporate a couple of more exotic or weird ingredients into one of your recipes and allow your guests to guess what they've eaten – sea slugs can be hugely popular!

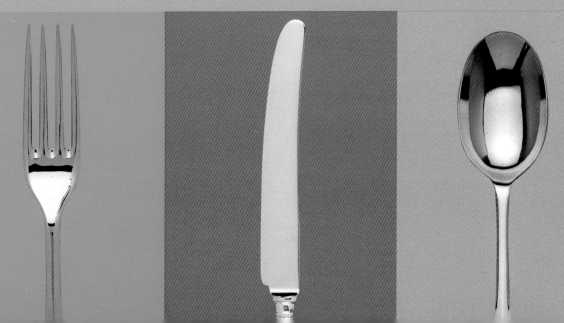

# Spatchcocked Poussin and Parmesan Patties

Poussin, fine green beans, semolina, Parmesan, mushrooms.

The only way to cook a whole poussin or chicken in 20 minutes is to 'spatchcock' the bird. It's quick, easy and it stays nice and juicy.

**SERVES 2**

400 g (14 oz) poussin
3 tablespoons olive oil
100 g (4 oz) fine green beans, chopped
250 g (9 oz) semolina
1 tablespoon chopped fresh basil
50 g (2 oz) Parmesan, freshly grated

**FOR THE MUSHROOM SAUCE**
150 ml (5 fl oz) double cream
100 g (4 oz) mushrooms, sliced
Juice of ½ lemon

**FOR THE DRESSING**
Juice of 1 lime
1 tablespoon clear honey
1 tablespoon Dijon mustard
1 teaspoon sesame oil
1 garlic clove, finely chopped
1 tablespoon double cream
2 tablespoons snipped fresh chives
1 tablespoon chopped fresh coriander
Salt and freshly ground black pepper
Fresh rosemary sprigs, to garnish

Pre-heat the oven to 220°C/425°F/Gas 7. Using kitchen scissors, cut along both sides of the backbone of the poussin and remove the backbone. Open out the poussin and flatten it with the heel of your hand. Season well with salt and pepper.

Heat 1 tablespoon of the olive oil in an ovenproof frying-pan and cook the poussin, skin-side down for 4 minutes. Transfer to the oven and cook for 20 minutes, turning once, until cooked through and golden brown.

Meanwhile, cook the beans in a pan of boiling salted water for 2–3 minutes until tender but still firm; drain and set aside.

To make the semolina patties, bring 600 ml (1 pint) of water to the boil and add the semolina, stirring continuously until thickened. Stir in the basil and three-quarters of the Parmesan; season to taste. Tip the mixture out on to a board and shape into two even-sized patties. Press a few of the chopped beans into one side of the patties.

Heat the remaining oil in a large frying-pan and cook the patties bean-side down for 2–3 minutes until golden brown. Turn and cook the other side. Remove from the pan and sprinkle over the remaining Parmesan.

To make the mushroom sauce, gently heat the cream in a small pan, add the mushrooms and cook for 2 minutes. Stir in the lemon juice and remaining beans and cook for a further 1–2 minutes; season to taste.

To make the dressing, stir together the lime juice, honey, mustard, sesame oil, garlic, double cream, chives and coriander in a small bowl. Add salt and pepper to taste.

To serve, pour the mushroom sauce on to a plate and place the patties in the centre. Place the poussin on top and drizzle over the dressing. Garnish with the rosemary.

You can use the spatchcock method to prepare any whole bird. It is also an ideal way of preparing poultry for the barbecue.

# ANTONY WORRALL THOMPSON
# Chicken Crème De La Crème

This simple dish of chicken in crème fraîche sauce with broccoli and sautéed vegetables makes a stylish after-work supper. The crème fraîche gives the sauce a delicious, tangy flavour.

Mustard seeds, shallots, potatoes, chicken breasts, long-grain rice, crème fraîche, broccoli.

Place the stock, garlic, parsley stalks, mustard seeds and shallots in a pan. Bring to the boil and simmer for 5 minutes. Add the potatoes and cook for a further 3 minutes. Add the chicken and cook for 10 minutes until both the potatoes and the chicken are tender. Drain the chicken and vegetables, reserving the poaching liquid. Discard the parsley stalks.

Cook the rice in a pan of boiling water for 10–12 minutes until the grains are tender.

Meanwhile, gently heat the crème fraîche and Worcestershire sauce in a small pan, without letting it boil. Stir in the mustard and wine and simmer together for 3 minutes. Gradually whisk in 150 ml (5 fl oz) of the poaching liquid, reducing between each addition, to give a smooth, glossy sauce. Season to taste.

Meanwhile, melt 25 g (1 oz) of butter in a large frying-pan and cook the poached shallots and potatoes for 3 minutes. Sprinkle over the sugar and cook for a further 3 minutes until tender and golden. Add salt and pepper to taste.

Cook the broccoli in a large pan of boiling salted water for 3–4 minutes until tender, then drain well. Stir t he poached chicken into the crème fraîche sauce and gently heat through.

Drain the rice and stir in the remaining butter. Spoon into two 10 cm (4 in) buttered ramekins, pressing down well.

To serve, turn out the rice on to a large serving plate. Place the broccoli in the centre and spoon the saucy chicken around the broccoli. Arrange the sautéed vegetables around the edge of the plate and garnish with the herbs.

If you don't have any crème fraîche to hand, you can still achieve a good, balanced sauce by using double cream and a squeeze of lemon juice.

## SERVES 2

600 ml (1 pint) hot chicken stock
4 garlic cloves
3–4 fresh parsley stalks
1 teaspoon mustard seeds
4 shallots
225 g (8 oz) potatoes, cut into 5 cm (2 in) chunks
2 x 175 g (6 oz) boneless, skinless chicken breasts
100 g (4 oz) long-grain rice
100 g (4 oz) crème fraîche
2 teaspoon Worcestershire sauce
2 teaspoons Dijon mustard
2 tablespoons white wine
75 g (3 oz) butter
1½ teaspoons caster sugar
175 g (6 oz) broccoli florets
Salt and freshly ground black pepper
Chopped fresh parsley and snipped fresh chives, to garnish

**RICHARD CAWLEY**

# What's up Duck?

Easy-cook long-grain rice, duck breasts, spring onions, red plums, asparagus tips, baby corn.

The combination of duck with fruit of all kinds is a classic, but usually involves more complicated dishes where the whole bird is traditionally roasted whole in the oven and the sauce made separately. This recipe, however, for duck with plums and pancakes, provides an effortless, elegant dish simply cooked in one pan on top of the stove.

### SERVES 4

700 ml (1¼ pints) hot vegetable stock
200 g (7 oz) easy-cook long-grain rice
Grated rind of 1 orange
2 tablespoons olive oil
2 x 350 g (12 oz) duck breasts
½ teaspoon ground cinnamon
1 bunch of spring onions, chopped
350 ml (12 fl oz) red wine
3 red plums, stoned and chopped
1 tablespoon demerara sugar
2 tablespoons self-raising flour
¼ teaspoon salt
½ teaspoon bicarbonate of soda
4 tablespoons milk
1 egg, beaten
1 tablespoon chopped fresh parsley
100 g (4 oz) asparagus tips
100 g (4 oz) baby corn
Salt and freshly ground black pepper

In a large pan, bring the stock to the boil and stir in the rice and orange rind. Bring back to the boil, then simmer for 12–15 minutes until the rice is tender. Drain and keep warm.

Meanwhile, heat ½ tablespoon of olive oil in a heavy-based frying-pan and add the duck, skin-side down. Sprinkle over the cinnamon and a third of the spring onions. Cook for 10 minutes, then turn. Add the red wine and the plums then sprinkle over the sugar and a little salt and pepper. Cover and cook gently for 10 minutes until the duck is cooked through.

Meanwhile, make the pancakes. Sift the flour, salt and bicarbonate of soda into a bowl. Whisk in the milk and beaten egg to make a smooth batter, then stir in the remaining spring onions and the parsley.

Heat ½ tablespoon of olive oil in a large frying-pan and cook the pancake batter, a tablespoonful at a time, for 2–3 minutes on each side until golden brown. Drain on kitchen paper.

Meanwhile, heat the remaining 1 tablespoon of olive oil in a griddle pan or heavy-based frying-pan and cook the asparagus and baby corn for 2–3 minutes until golden and tender.

To serve, place the pancakes on a plate and spoon over the vegetables. Top with the duck breasts and sauce.

There are many ways of cooking rice, but the simplest, foolproof method is to wash the rice very thoroughly in a sieve under a cold running tap until the water runs clear, then boil in plenty of salted water, without stirring, until just tender. Drain in a sieve and serve immediately.

# Tex Mex Turkey

Tinned kidney beans or pinto beans, spring onions, green pepper, tinned chopped tomatoes, turkey breast stir-fry strips, plain chocolate, flour tortillas, pickled green Jalapeño chillies.

No need to travel down Mexico way for this free-style interpretation of Mexican burritos, for which I mercilessly plundered the **Ready Steady Cook** larder. It's packed with eating excitement!

**SERVES 2**

4 spring onions

FOR THE RE-FRIED BEANS
40 g (1½ oz) butter
400 g tin of kidney beans or pinto beans, drained
1 teaspoon ground cumin
¼ teaspoon hot chilli powder

FOR THE CHILLI
1 tablespoon sunflower oil
15 g (½ oz) butter
2 spring onions, sliced
½ green pepper, seeded and chopped
200 g tin of chopped tomatoes
1 tablespoon tomato purée
225 g (8 oz) turkey breast stir-fry strips
1 teaspoon ground cumin
¼ teaspoon hot chilli powder
1 teaspoon dried oregano
½ teaspoon cocoa powder or 2 small squares plain chocolate, grated
3 tablespoons double cream
2 teaspoons lemon juice
Salt and freshly ground black pepper

TO SERVE
6 soft flour tortillas
150 g (5 oz) Greek yoghurt
1 tablespoon chopped, pickled, green Jalapeño chillies
Fresh flatleaf parsley sprigs, to garnish

To make the spring onion garnish, cut away the green parts to leave a 5 cm (2 in) length with the root still intact. Thinly slice each spring onion lengthways without cutting through the root. Put the lengths in a bowl of iced water and set them aside to curl.

To make the re-fried beans, melt the butter in a heavy-based frying-pan and add the kidney beans. Mash with a potato masher to form a coarse purée. Stir in the cumin, chilli powder and salt and pepper to taste. Cook gently for 10 minutes, stirring occasionally, until piping hot.

Meanwhile, make the chilli filling. Heat the oil and butter in a separate, heavy-based frying-pan and cook the sliced spring onions and chopped pepper for 2 minutes. Stir in the chopped tomatoes and tomato purée, then push the mixture to one side of the pan. Place the turkey in the other side of the pan and stir in the cumin and chilli, oregano, cocoa powder or chocolate and salt and pepper. Cook for 2–3 minutes, then stir together the turkey and vegetables and cook for a further 8 minutes until the vegetables are tender and the turkey is cooked through. Stir in the cream and lemon juice and cook for 1 minute.

Heat the tortillas, one at a time, in a hot, dry frying-pan for 1–2 minutes, turning once.

To serve, mix together the yoghurt and chopped chillies and spoon into a small serving bowl. Fold two of the tortillas into quarters and place them on the side of a serving plate. Roll up another tortilla and place this in the centre of the plate. Spoon half of the turkey chilli over the central tortilla and spoon two piles of re-fried beans next to the quartered tortillas. Repeat for the second plate. Garnish with the spring onion tassels and flatleaf parsley.

I always keep flour tortillas in my store cupboard – they come in handy for all sorts of things. To make them soft enough for rolling, just pop in a hot non-stick frying-pan for a few seconds on each side, or alternatively microwave for about 30 seconds.

**PHIL VICKERY**

# Running Rings Round Duck

Some of my personal favourites are combined in this dish of glazed duck with couscous and onion rings. I really enjoy cooking duck and these are the best ever onion rings.

Couscous, duck leg portions, pumpkin seeds, dried apricots, onion, green beans.

Pre-heat the oven to 200°C/400°F/Gas 6. Place the couscous and herbs in a large bowl and pour over the boiling water. Set aside for 10 minutes until the grains have absorbed the water.

Score the duck skin and sprinkle with the ground ginger, cumin and a little salt and pepper. Heat a non-stick griddle pan or heavy-based frying-pan and cook the duck skin-side down for 5 minutes until browned. Transfer to an ovenproof dish and roast for 5 minutes. Baste the duck with the pan juices, then return to the oven for a further 5 minutes. Drizzle over a quarter of the lime juice and the honey and return to the oven for a further 5–10 minutes until the duck is cooked through. Remove the duck from the oven, cover and set aside to rest.

Meanwhile, stir two-thirds of the remaining lime juice, the chopped apricots, 2 tablespoons of the olive oil and 1 tablespoon of the pumpkin seeds into the couscous.

Dip the onion rings into the milk and then the flour, then repeat the process twice, until the rings are well coated. Deep-fry in the hot oil for 5 minutes until crisp and golden brown; drain on kitchen paper.

Heat the remaining tablespoon of olive oil in a frying-pan and stir-fry the garlic and beans for 2 minutes. Stir in the remaining pumpkin seeds and stir-fry for a further 2 minutes until the beans are tender. Stir in the remaining lime juice, and add salt and pepper to taste.

To serve, spoon the couscous on to a large plate and arrange the glazed duck on top. Garnish with the stir-fried beans and the crispy onion rings.

Couscous is a grain made from ground durum wheat. It is rolled in fine flour to keep the grains separate during cooking and is usually available partially cooked so it only needs soaking in hot water to rehydrate the grains.

**SERVES 2**

100 g (4 oz) couscous
4 tablespoons chopped fresh herbs, e.g. mint, coriander, chives, parsley
300 ml (10 fl oz) boiling water
2 x 225 g (8 oz) duck leg portions, boned
1 teaspoon ground ginger
1 teaspoon ground cumin
Juice of 2 limes
1 tablespoon clear honey
50 g (2 oz) ready-to-eat dried apricots, roughly chopped
3 tablespoons olive oil
4 tablespoons pumpkin seeds, toasted
1 onion, sliced into rings
150 ml (5 fl oz) milk
4 tablespoons plain flour
Vegetable oil, for deep-frying
1 garlic clove, crushed
100 g (4 oz) green beans, halved widthways
Salt and freshly ground black pepper

**ANTHONY TOBIN**

# Grand Guinea Fowl with Grape Dressing

Potatoes, guinea fowl breasts, red pepper, shallots, seedless green grapes.

This simple but very stylish dish would serve as a lovely dinner-party main course. The dressing can be prepared several hours in advance.

### SERVES 2

2 potatoes, cut into 2.5 cm (1 in) thick slices
3 tablespoons olive oil
2 x 75 g (3 oz) boneless guinea fowl breasts
1 red pepper
2 shallots, quartered

### FOR THE GRAPE DRESSING

25 g (1 oz) butter
25 g (1 oz) caster sugar
½ tablespoon balsamic vinegar
½ tablespoon red wine vinegar
Sprig of fresh basil
2 tablespoons olive oil
50 g (2 oz) seedless green grapes, halved
Salt and freshly ground black pepper
Fresh basil leaves, to garnish

Pre-heat the oven to 200°C/400°F/Gas 6. Cook the potato slices in a large pan of boiling salted water for 5–8 minutes until just tender, then drain well.

Heat 1 tablespoon of the oil in a skillet or ovenproof frying-pan and cook the breasts for 4–5 minutes, turning once until golden. Season well, then place the pan in the hot oven for 5–6 minutes until the meat is cooked through.

Meanwhile, cut the pepper into quarters and neaten up into even-sized pieces; reserve the trimmings but discard the seeds. Heat the remaining oil in large griddle pan or heavy-based frying-pan. Cook the shallots, pepper quarters and potato slices for 4–5 minutes on each side until tender and golden brown.

Meanwhile, make the grape dressing. Heat the butter in a small frying-pan and add the reserved pepper trimmings and the caster sugar. Cook gently, stirring frequently, for 5–6 minutes until the peppers have softened and browned. Stir in the vinegars and bring to the boil, then pour the mixture into a bowl. Add the basil and olive oil and set aside to cool. Strain into a clean bowl and stir in the grapes; season to taste.

To serve, arrange the griddled vegetables on a large serving plate and place the guinea fowl breasts on top. Spoon round the dressing and garnish with the basil leaves.

Guinea fowl has a very mild gamey flavour and the breasts are ideal for speedy cooking methods such as frying, grilling, barbecuing and quick-roasting in a hot oven. They can be substituted in this dish with small corn-fed chicken breasts.

# Quail Without Fail

Quails, onion, celery, tomatoes, sultanas, couscous.

This spectacular and delicious recipe for spatchcocked quail with couscous brings together all kinds of different ethnic influences reflecting our growing appetite for more exotic flavours. The quails cook to perfection under the grill but taste even better when cooked over glowing charcoal in the barbecue season.

**SERVES 2**

2 quails
Juice of 1 lime
1 tablespoon soy sauce
1 tablespoon clear honey
1 tablespoon sesame oil
Few drops of Tabasco sauce
2 garlic cloves, crushed
2 tablespoons sunflower oil
1 onion, chopped
2 celery sticks, chopped
600 ml (1 pint) chicken stock
4 tomatoes, each cut into 8 wedges
50 g (2 oz) sultanas
25 g (1 oz) butter
175 g (6 oz) couscous
Salt and freshly ground black pepper
Snipped fresh chives, to garnish

Using kitchen scissors, cut along both sides of the backbone of each quail and remove the backbone. Open out the quails and flatten them with the heel of your hand. Push two 20 cm (8 in) skewers diagonally through each quail. (If using bamboo skewers, soak them in hot water for at least 30 minutes before use to stop them burning during cooking.)

Mix together the lime juice, soy sauce, honey, sesame oil, Tabasco, half the garlic, and salt and pepper to taste. Brush the quails with the mixture and cook under a pre-heated medium grill for 12–15 minutes, turning once and basting occasionally with any remaining mixture, until cooked and well browned.

Meanwhile, heat the sunflower oil in a pan and cook the onion, celery and remaining garlic for 3 minutes until softened. Stir in 150 ml (5 fl oz) of the stock, the tomatoes, sultanas, a few more drops of Tabasco, and salt and pepper to taste. Bring to the boil, then simmer for 5 minutes.

Melt the butter in a pan and stir in the couscous, remaining stock and a little salt and pepper. Bring to the boil then simmer for 3–4 minutes until the couscous grains are light and fluffy.

To serve, spoon the celery mixture on to a plate and top with the couscous. Arrange the grilled quail on top of the couscous and garnish with the chives.

Quails are now extensively farmed and are available in most supermarkets for a reasonable price. In taste and texture, they are very similar to young chicken. A good substitute would be poussins split in half, although this would provide a more substantial and slightly less elegant dish.

ROSS BURDEN

# Awesome Ostrich

The texture and flavour of ostrich is that of lemony fillet steak – well worth trying. In this recipe, it is served with potato galettes, stuffed mushrooms and a delicious red-wine sauce.

 Savoy cabbage leaves, carrots, ostrich steak, onion, chopped fresh tarragon, flat mushrooms, red-skinned potatoes.

Pre-heat the oven to 200°C/400°F/Gas 6. Cook the cabbage leaves in a large pan of boiling salted water for 2 minutes. Add the carrot ribbons and cook for a further 1 minute. Drain well, then cool under cold water and set aside.

Heat 1 tablespoon of the olive oil in a large frying-pan and cook the ostrich steak for 1–2 minutes on each side until well browned. Remove from the pan and wrap the carrot ribbons around the steak, then wrap the cabbage leaves around them and secure with cocktail sticks. Place on a baking sheet and cook for 10 minutes. For a well-done steak cook for 15 minutes.

Heat ½ tablespoon of olive oil in the frying-pan and cook the onion for 3–4 minutes, until softened.

Meanwhile, make the stuffed mushrooms. Blend the bread in a food processor until it forms crumbs. Transfer to a bowl and stir in the tarragon, half the cooked onion, ½ tablespoon of olive oil and plenty of salt and pepper. Remove the stalks from the mushrooms and stuff the cups with the crumb mixture. Bake for 8-10 minutes until the mushrooms are tender and the filling is golden.

Heat the remaining 2 tablespoons of olive oil in a large frying-pan. Shape the sliced potatoes into galettes by overlapping them to make two circular discs. Cook for 2–3 minutes on each side until golden brown and cooked through.

Meanwhile, pour the red wine into the pan of remaining onion and crumble in the stock cube. Add the vinegar and sugar, season to taste and simmer for 2–3 minutes, stirring to dissolve the stock cube. Sieve the sauce into a clean pan and warm through.

To serve, flood the base of two plates with the sauce and place a potato galette in the centre. Slice the ostrich steak in half diagonally, remove and discard the cocktail sticks and arrange the steaks on top of the potato galettes. Garnish the stuffed mushrooms with the parsley sprigs and serve on a separate plate.

 This unusual meat is finding great favour with people who enjoy red meat but want to cut down on saturated fat and cholesterol – it has around half the fat of beef. As it is such a lean meat, it is best served rare, still pink.

## SERVES 2

6 large Savoy cabbage leaves
2 carrots, cut into ribbons with a vegetable peeler
4 tablespoons olive oil
200 g (7 oz) ostrich steak
1 onion, finely chopped
3 slices of country-style white bread
2 tablespoons chopped fresh tarragon
3 flat mushrooms
2 red-skinned potatoes, unpeeled, thinly sliced
100 ml (3½ fl oz) red wine
1 vegetable stock cube
1 tablespoon balsamic vinegar
1 teaspoon brown sugar
Salt and freshly ground black pepper
Fresh flatleaf parsley sprigs, to garnish

**BRIAN TURNER**

# Very Pleasant Pheasant with Bubble and Squeak

Bubble and squeak with sprouts, pheasant and chestnuts make for very exciting eating.

Pheasant breasts, chestnuts, tinned blackcurrants, redcurrant jelly, potatoes, Brussels sprouts, onion, brandy.

Pre-heat the oven to 200°C/400°F/Gas 6. To make the stuffing, heat the oil in a pan and stir in the chestnuts, blackcurrants and redcurrant jelly. Cook for 2–3 minutes until the mixture is thick and pasty, then leave to cool.

Place the pheasant in a buttered ovenproof dish and season well. Mix together the cream, wine and mustard and spread the mixture over the pheasant breasts. Roast for 8 minutes, basting occasionally. Remove from the oven and using a small knife cut a pocket in each breast. Pack the cavities with the stuffing, piling any excess mixture on top, and return the pheasant to the oven for 5 minutes until cooked through.

Meanwhile, make the bubble and squeak. Cook the potatoes in a large pan of boiling water for 5 minutes. Add the Brussels and cook for a further 5 minutes until both vegetables are tender. Drain well and mash together, seasoning with salt and pepper. Heat the oil in a large heavy-based frying-pan and cook the mixture for 5–6 minutes, turning once until well browned.

To make the brandy sauce, heat the oil in a separate frying-pan and cook the onion for 5 minutes until softened. Stir in the stock, brandy, cream, parsley and dill, bring to the boil, then simmer rapidly until reduced by two-thirds; season to taste.

To serve, spoon the bubble and squeak on to a large plate and arrange the pheasant on top. Pour over the sauce and garnish with the parsley and dill sprigs.

Pheasant is in season from 1st October to 1st February. Take care when cooking it as the meat is lean and prone to drying out.

SERVES 2

2 pheasant breasts
1 tablespoon double cream
2 teaspoons dry white wine
1 teaspoon Dijon mustard

FOR THE STUFFING
2 tablespoons sunflower oil
100 g (4 oz) cooked chestnuts, roughly chopped
½ x 275 g tin of blackcurrants, drained
1 tablespoon redcurrant jelly

FOR THE BUBBLE AND SQUEAK
350 g (12 oz) potatoes, diced
75 g (3 oz) Brussels sprouts, halved
2 tablespoons sunflower oil

FOR THE BRANDY SAUCE
1 tablespoon sunflower oil
1 small onion, finely chopped
300 ml (10 fl oz) chicken stock
2 tablespoons brandy
150 ml (5 fl oz) double cream
1 tablespoon chopped fresh parsley
1 tablespoon chopped fresh dill
Salt and freshly ground black pepper
Fresh parsley and dill sprigs, to garnish

# Fruity Rabbit and Mixed Mash

Red-skinned potato, parsnip, fine green beans, dried ready-to-eat prunes, rabbit, onion.

This delicious and rather unusual dish makes the most of rabbit, a very underestimated meat. You could, however, substitute chicken very successfully. The fruity sauce made with caramelized prunes adds a real 'chef's' touch to this deceptively simple recipe.

### SERVES 2

100 ml (3½ fl oz ) white wine
1 red-skinned potato, diced
1 parsnip, diced
100 g (4 oz) butter
Juice of 1 orange
4 tablespoons olive oil
75 g (3 oz) fine green beans
2 teaspoons granulated sugar
2 tablespoons water
2 tablespoons white wine vinegar
3 tablespoons double cream
50 g (2 oz) dried ready-to-eat prunes
350 g (12 oz) rabbit, cut into bite-sized pieces
1 onion, chopped
1 garlic clove, crushed
Salt and freshly ground black pepper

Pour the wine into a pan and then half fill with water. Bring to the boil, add the potato and parsnip and cook for 10–12 minutes until tender. Drain well and mash with three-quarters of the butter and plenty of salt and pepper.

Meanwhile, make the dressing. Stir together the orange juice and 3 tablespoons of olive oil, adding salt and pepper to taste. Blanch the beans in a pan of boiling salted water for 1–2 minutes until tender but still firm. Drain well and toss with the dressing; set aside.

Place the sugar and water in a small pan and cook gently, without stirring, until the sugar melts and the mixture turns into golden caramel. Stir in the wine vinegar, then after 30 seconds add the cream and prunes. Remove from the heat.

Meanwhile, heat the remaining butter and olive oil in a frying-pan and cook the rabbit pieces for 2 minutes until browned. Add the onion and garlic and cook for a further 5 minutes until the onion is softened and the rabbit is cooked through.

To serve, pile the mash in the centre of a plate and place the rabbit pieces on top. Arrange the beans around the mash and pour over the caramelized sauce.

For a successful caramel, use a small, good-quality non-stick pan and leave the mixture undisturbed over the heat just until it reaches the desired caramel colour. To stop the cooking at this stage, hold the bottom of the pan in a large bowl of cold water to lower the temperature quickly.

**RICHARD CAWLEY**

# Venison Cuts the Mustard

A fabulous fast dish, this recipe for venison with sautéed vegetables and Dijon mustard sauce has a real taste of luxury. Venison is a very lean, healthy meat and is now available in most large supermarkets.

 Venison steaks, onion, potato, marrow, fresh rosemary sprigs, salad leaves.

Cover the venison in clingfilm and bat with a rolling pin to flatten out. Cut the steaks into 5 mm (¼ in) strips.

Heat 1 tablespoon of the olive oil in a frying-pan and add the venison strips. Cook over a high heat for 3–4 minutes on each side. Remove with a slotted spoon and transfer to an ovenproof dish; keep warm in a low oven.

Add half the onion to the same frying-pan and cook for 3–4 minutes until softened. Add the wine and cook over a high heat for 3 minutes. Stir in the butter, mustard, honey and Worcestershire sauce and cook for 3–4 minutes. Mix together the yoghurt and water and stir into the pan. Heat through gently without boiling.

Meanwhile, heat the remaining oil in a wok and stir-fry the potato, marrow, remaining onion, rosemary and parsley for 4–5 minutes until tender. Add salt and pepper to taste.

To serve, spoon the sautéed vegetables on a plate and arrange the venison strips on top. Spoon over the sauce and serve with salad.

Many people are nervous of eating venison either because they think it will taste too strong and gamey or because of sentimental reasons. Modern venison is not hung as long as it was traditionally and hence has no stronger a flavour than good beef. As for sentimentality, it is absolutely necessary to cull the ever-increasing population of deer in Scotland in order to save the natural habitat of the highlands from destruction.

SERVES 2

2 x 225 g (8 oz) venison steaks
3 tablespoons olive oil
1 onion, finely chopped
5 tablespoons white wine
Small knob of butter
1 teaspoon Dijon mustard
1 teaspoon clear honey
½ teaspoon Worcestershire sauce
2 teaspoons Greek yoghurt
2 tablespoons water
1 potato, diced
¼ marrow, seeded and cut into fine, 5 mm (¼ in) long strips
2 fresh rosemary sprigs
1 tablespoon chopped fresh parsley
Salt and freshly ground black pepper
Salad leaves, to serve

# MEAT DISHES

# Mini Beef Wellingtons with Béarnaise Sauce

Chicken livers, shallots, button mushrooms, plum tomatoes, brandy, ready-rolled puff pastry, fillet steaks, small patty-pan squashes.

This is an adaptation of a classic dish. It's a great dinner-party dish as the beef wellingtons can be made the day before and freshly baked prior to serving. *Illustrated on page 118.*

### SERVES 2

100 g (4 oz) chicken livers
2 shallots, roughly chopped
1 tablespoon chopped fresh parsley
4 button mushrooms, roughly chopped
1 plum tomato, skinned and chopped
1 garlic clove
1–2 tablespoons brandy
2 tablespoons olive oil
375 g pack ready rolled puff pastry
2 x 150–175 g (5–6 oz) fillet steaks
1 tablespoon French or Dijon mustard
1 egg yolk, beaten

### FOR THE SAUCE

2 egg yolks
1 tablespoon white wine
75 g (3 oz) unsalted butter, melted
1 tablespoon chopped fresh parsley
1 tablespoon chopped fresh coriander

### FOR THE BUTTERED VEGETABLES

25 g (1 oz) butter
6 button mushrooms
2 small patty-pan squashes, seeded and quartered
Salt and freshly ground black pepper

1 plum tomato, chopped, and fresh dill sprigs, to garnish

Pre-heat the oven to 220°C/425°F/Gas 7. Place the chicken livers, shallots, parsley, mushrooms, tomato, garlic and brandy in a food processor and whizz until smooth. Season with salt and pepper. Heat 1 tablespoon of the olive oil in a pan, pour in the mixture and cook for 5–6 minutes until thickened.

Cut two 20 cm (8 in) squares out of the pastry.

Using a rolling pin or meat mallet, flatten the steaks to a thickness of 5 cm (2 in). Heat the remaining oil in a separate heavy-based frying-pan and cook the steaks for 1 minute on each side until well browned.

Place a steak in the centre of each pastry square, season, then spread with mustard. Spoon the chicken liver mixture on top. Brush the edges of the pastry with the beaten egg yolk, then fold over to enclose the filling, pressing down well to seal. Place the parcels joint-side down on a baking sheet and brush with the remaining egg yolk. Bake for 15 minutes until the pastry is puffed and golden.

Meanwhile, make the Béarnaise sauce. Place the egg yolks in a heatproof bowl and sit the bowl over a pan of simmering water. Add the wine and whisk until the mixture is thick enough to leave a trail. Gradually whisk in the melted butter to make a thick, foaming sauce. Add the parsley and coriander.

To cook the buttered vegetables, melt the butter in a frying-pan and sauté the mushrooms and patty-pan squashes for 4–5 minutes until tender and golden; season with salt and pepper.

To serve, place the beef parcels on plates and garnish with the chopped plum tomato and dill sprigs. Spoon the buttered vegetables on to the plate and spoon round the sauce.

When making an emulsified sauce, such as mayonnaise or Béarnaise, the oil or melted butter is whisked into an egg yolk which coats each fat droplet; this prevents the oil droplets from sticking together in one pool of liquid and results in a thickened, glossy sauce. It is important that the melted butter is added very gradually or the egg will not be properly dispersed and the mixture can curdle.

**PATRICK ANTHONY**

# Steak and Pasta Ribbons in Mushroom Sauce

Another dish that the studio crew rushed to try as soon as we stopped recording – always a good sign! The simple and delicious ingredients were easy to prepare and even easier to eat – an unbeatable combination.

 Pappardelle (broad pasta ribbons) or tagliatelle, rump steak, onion, red pepper, green pepper, mushrooms.

Cook the pasta in a large pan of boiling salted water for 10–12 minutes until tender. Drain well and toss with 1 tablespoon of the oil.

Meanwhile, heat the butter and remaining oil in a large heavy-based frying-pan and cook the steak and onion for 3–4 minutes until browned. Remove with a slotted spoon and set aside.

Add the peppers, garlic, mustard, parsley, Worcestershire sauce and wine to the same pan and bring to the boil, then simmer for 3–4 minutes. Stir in the mushrooms, cooked onions and steak, then add the cream and cook for 1–2 minutes; season to taste.

To serve, toss together the pasta and sauce and sprinkle over the chopped parsley.

There's no need to wash commercially produced mushrooms as they are grown on sterile material. Just a quick wipe with a damp cloth will do if needed.

## SERVES 2

175 g (6 oz) pappardelle (broad pasta ribbons) or tagliatelle
2 tablespoons olive oil
25 g (1 oz) butter
225 g (8 oz) rump steak, cut into thin strips
½ onion, finely chopped
1 red pepper, seeded and diced
1 green pepper, seeded and diced
1 garlic clove, finely chopped
1 teaspoon Dijon mustard
1 tablespoon chopped fresh parsley
Few drops of Worcestershire sauce
5 tablespoons white wine
100 g (4 oz) mushrooms, sliced
4 tablespoons double cream
Salt and freshly ground black pepper
Chopped fresh parsley, to garnish

# BRIAN TURNER'S
# Five Favourite Sauces

The essence of great sauce-making is the blending of fresh flavours into a liquid of a consistency and colour that is attractive and tasteful when poured on, over or round its accompanying food. A real sauce will complement the flavours and textures of the food on the plate, giving an added quality to the food whilst not distracting from the food's original flavours. For many sauces, the basic liquid added is a stock which is a thin liquid with the combined flavours of various vegetables or a blend of vegetables, herbs and bones – either meat, fish or chicken.

**Bordelaise Sauce** This is brilliant served with thick steaks. Place 2 finely chopped shallots and a glass of red wine in a pan and bring to the boil; simmer rapidly until reduced by half. Stir in 300 ml (10 fl oz) of beef stock, return to the boil and simmer for a further 5 minutes. Stir in 50 g (2 oz) of diced bone marrow and a teaspoon of chopped fresh parsley. Season to taste and serve immediately.

**Chasseur Sauce** Good with meat and poultry, especially chicken. Melt a large knob of butter in pan and cook 450 g (1 lb) of sliced mushrooms until tender and golden. Stir a small, crushed garlic clove, a chopped shallot and a glass of white wine; bring to the boil and simmer rapidly until reduced by half. Stir in 8 skinned, seeded and chopped tomatoes and a teaspoon of chopped fresh tarragon and cook for 3 minutes. Stir in 150 ml (5 fl oz) of veal stock and simmer for 10 minutes. Add salt and pepper to taste, stir in a teaspoon of chopped fresh parsley and serve immediately.

**Sauce Ravigote** This simple sauce is delicious with fish, cold meats and salad. Whisk together 1 tablespoon of white wine vinegar, 3 tablespoons of olive oil, 1 tablespoon of Dijon mustard, 1 tablespoon of finely chopped spring onions, 1 chopped, hard-boiled egg, 1 tablespoon of chopped, fresh, mixed herbs (parsley, tarragon, chervil) and salt and pepper to taste.

**Sauce Robert** Great with pork, beef and chicken. Melt a large knob of butter in a pan and cook half a chopped onion for 5 minutes until softened. Stir in a glass of dry white wine, bring to the boil and simmer rapidly until reduced by half. Stir in 1 tablespoon of white wine vinegar, 300 ml (10 fl oz) of beef stock, 50 g (2 oz) of chopped gherkins, 1 teaspoon of Dijon mustard, 25 g (1 oz) of capers and a teaspoon of chopped fresh parsley. Season to taste and serve.

**Rich Rum Sauce** This is fantastic with steamed puddings, especially Christmas pudding. Place 300 ml (10 fl oz) of milk and the same of double cream in a pan with a halved vanilla pod; slowly bring to the boil. In a heatproof bowl, whisk together 5 egg yolks, 100 g (4 oz) of caster sugar and 25 g (1 oz) of plain flour. Whisk the milk in to the egg yolk mixture, then return to a clean pan and bring back to the boil, stirring constantly to make a smooth, glossy sauce. Remove from the heat and stir in 150 ml (5 fl oz) of double cream (lightly whipped) and a splash of dark rum to taste.

**PHIL VICKERY**

# Smashing Hash and Sweetcorn Fritters

Onion, tinned corned beef, brown sauce, tinned chopped tomatoes, tinned sweetcorn with peppers, dried instant mash potato.

As a child, I loved corned beef hash – it still reminds me of my Auntie Joey who makes the best hash ever.

### SERVES 2

2 tablespoons vegetable oil
½ onion, finely chopped
1 garlic clove, crushed
340 g tin of corned beef, roughly chopped
Grated rind and juice of ½ orange
1 tablespoon brown sauce
2 teaspoons Worcestershire sauce
400 g tin of chopped tomatoes
2 tablespoons chopped fresh basil
2 eggs
100 g (4 oz) self-raising flour
6 tablespoons milk
200 g tin of sweetcorn with peppers, drained
175 g (6 oz) dried instant mashed potato
750 ml (1¼ pints) boiling water
Knob of butter
Salt and freshly ground black pepper
Fresh dill sprigs, to garnish

Heat 1 tablespoon of the oil in a small pan and cook the onion and garlic for 5 minutes until softened.

In a large bowl, mix together the corned beef, orange rind and juice. Add to the pan of onions along with the brown sauce and half the Worcestershire sauce and cook for 3–4 minutes, stirring until warmed through. Add salt and pepper to taste, cover and keep warm.

In a small pan, gently heat the chopped tomatoes. Stir in the basil, remaining Worcestershire sauce and salt and pepper to taste. Using a hand blender, whizz the mixture until smooth; keep warm.

In a large bowl, whisk together the eggs and flour, then gradually beat in half the milk to make a smooth, thick batter. Stir in the sweetcorn and salt and pepper to taste.

Heat the remaining tablespoon of oil in a large heavy-based frying-pan and sit four 4 cm (1½ in) rings in the pan. Ladle the batter into the rings to make rounds about 2.5 cm (1 in) thick. Cook for 2 minutes until the underside is golden, then turn over the fritters and cook for a further 2 minutes until puffed and golden.

Place the instant mashed potato in a large bowl and pour over the boiling water, stirring continuously. Beat in the remaining 3 tablespoons of milk, the butter and salt and pepper to taste. Spoon the potato mixture into a piping bag.

To serve, spoon the hash on to serving plates and pipe the potato over the top. Arrange the fritters on the potato and garnish with the dill. Spoon round the tomato sauce and serve.

Convenience foods like instant potato and gravy granules are really handy to have in your store cupboard – especially for us scatter-brained chefs.

# THANE PRINCE
# Full of Eastern Promise

Don't feel intimidated by oriental cookery – this yummy dish of Chinese-style beef and noodles with a red wine glaze and aubergine fritters is simplicity itself.

Chinese-style egg noodles, star anise, rump steak, aubergine, spring onions, red pepper, sesame seeds, Chinese five-spice powder.

Cook the noodles in large pan of boiling water for 4–5 minutes until tender; drain well.

Place the star anise, garlic and a pinch of salt in a pestle and mortar and pound together to make a paste. Stir in 4 tablespoons of the soy sauce, then pour the mixture over the steak, turning to coat; set aside to marinate.

To make the glaze, stir together the tomato purée, red wine, five-spice powder and lime juice to taste in a small pan. Bring to the boil and simmer rapidly for 5 minutes until reduced and shiny; stir in the shredded basil leaves.

To make the aubergine fritters, heat the vegetable oil in a large, heavy-based frying-pan. Dip the aubergine slices in the seasoned flour, then the beaten egg. Cook for 2–3 minutes on each side until tender and golden brown. Drain on kitchen paper and keep warm.

For the stir-fry, heat the vegetable oil in a wok or large frying-pan and stir-fry the aubergine, spring onion and pepper strips over a high heat for 5–6 minutes until tender but still firm. Stir in the noodles, sesame seeds, sesame oil and remaining 2 tablespoons of soy sauce. Continue to cook for 1–2 minutes until piping hot.

Meanwhile, cook the steak in a non-stick griddle or heavy-based pan for 3–4 minutes on each side until well browned but still a little pink in the centre. Remove the steak from the pan and slice into 1 cm (½ in) thick strips. Stir any remaining marinade into the red wine glaze and continue to boil for a further 1–2 minutes; check the seasoning.

To serve, spoon the noodles on to a serving dish and arrange the steak strips on top. Place the aubergine fritters next to the noodles and drizzle round the red wine glaze. Garnish with the lime wedges and basil leaves.

## SERVES 2

200 g (7 oz) Chinese-style egg noodles
1 star anise
1 large garlic clove
6 tablespoons soy sauce
200 g (7 oz) rump steak
1 tablespoon vegetable oil
½ aubergine, cut into 1 cm (½ in) strips
1 bunch of spring onions, quartered lengthways
1 red pepper, seeded and sliced into 1 cm (½ in) wide strips
1 tablespoon sesame seeds
1 tablespoon sesame oil

### FOR THE RED WINE GLAZE
1 tablespoon tomato purée
150 ml (5 fl oz) red wine
½ teaspoon Chinese five-spice powder
Juice of 1 lime
1 tablespoon shredded fresh basil

### FOR THE FRITTERS
2 tablespoons vegetable oil
½ aubergine, thinly sliced into 5 mm (¼ in) rounds
3 tablespoons seasoned plain flour
1 egg, beaten
Salt and freshly ground black pepper

Lime wedges and fresh basil leaves, to garnish

Develop the flavour of the dish by marinating the steak overnight.

# Steak 'n' Salsa Sarnie

Tinned chopped tomatoes, red chilli, avocados, sesame pitta breads, onion, tinned kidney beans, rump steak

This hot beef sandwich with tomato and avocado salsa makes a perfect speedy and filling lunch or late supper. Store any remaining salsa in an airtight container for up to 24 hours and serve with toasted strips of pitta as a Mexican-style snack.

**SERVES 2**

**FOR THE SALSA**
400 g tin of chopped tomatoes
Juice of 1 lime
1 tablespoon tomato purée
1 teaspoon balsamic vinegar
Few drops of Tabasco
1 red chilli, seeded and finely chopped
1 tablespoon chopped fresh basil
1 garlic clove, finely chopped
1–2 teaspoons caster sugar
2 ripe avocados, skinned, stoned and diced

**FOR THE PITTA BREAD**
2 sesame pitta breads
2 tablespoons olive oil

**FOR THE BEANS**
1 tablespoon vegetable oil
1 onion, finely chopped
1 tablespoon chopped fresh coriander
400 g tin of kidney beans, drained
1 tablespoon olive oil

**FOR THE STEAK**
1 tablespoon vegetable oil
350 g (12 oz) rump steak
1 garlic clove, finely chopped
Salt and freshly ground black pepper

Fresh basil leaves, to garnish

Pre-heat the oven to 200°C/400°F/Gas 6. Begin by making the salsa. Place the chopped tomatoes in a pan with the lime juice and bring to the boil. Stir in the tomato purée, vinegar, Tabasco, chilli, chopped basil, garlic and sugar and salt and pepper to taste and simmer for 5 minutes. Stir in the avocado and cook for a further 3–4 minutes.

Meanwhile, split open the pitta breads and place on a baking sheet, brush with the olive oil and bake for 5–6 minutes until golden.

To make the bean filling, heat 1 tablespoon of the vegetable oil in a frying-pan and cook the onion for 5 minutes, until softened. Stir in the coriander and kidney beans, season and cook for 5 minutes. Transfer to a bowl and drizzle over the olive oil.

To cook the steak, heat the vegetable oil in a griddle pan or heavy-based frying-pan. Halve the steak horizontally, then season well with salt and pepper and sprinkle over the garlic. Cook the steak in the hot griddle pan for 2–3 minutes on each side until well browned but still a little pink in the centre.

To serve, place two bottom halves of baked pitta on a plate and spoon a tablespoon of the salsa on top of each. Place the meat on top then place the remaining seeded pitta halves over the meat to make two sandwiches. Serve hot.

The preparation time of this recipe can be cut right back by using one of the commercially made fresh salsas now available from delicatessens and supermarkets.

# Stuffed Steak and Potato Pancakes

Shallots, rump steaks, potato, parsnip, savoy cabbage leaves.

This dish of stuffed and rolled beef, traditionally known as beef olives, is a real classic and the curried potato pancakes offer a modern twist.

**SERVES 2**

50 g (2 oz) butter
3–4 tablespoons olive oil
100 g (4 oz) shallots, quartered
2 x 150 g (5 oz) rump steaks
1 tablespoon white wine
1 large potato, grated
1 parsnip, grated
1 teaspoon curry powder
4 Savoy cabbage leaves, finely shredded
3 garlic cloves, finely chopped
5 tablespoons double cream
Salt and freshly ground black pepper
Fresh coriander sprigs, to garnish

Heat half the butter and 1 tablespoon of olive oil in a pan and cook the shallots for 8 minutes, shaking the pan frequently until tender and golden.

Put the steaks between two sheets of clingfilm and flatten with a rolling pin until 5 mm (¼ in) thick. Spoon the shallots on top of the steaks, roll up and secure with cocktail sticks.

Heat the remaining butter and 1 tablespoon of olive oil in the same frying-pan and quickly brown the steak rolls. Add the wine and cook gently for 6 minutes, turning occasionally.

Meanwhile, make the potato pancakes. Mix together the grated potato, parsnips, curry powder and plenty of salt and pepper. Heat 1 tablespoon of olive oil in a large heavy-based frying-pan. Sit four 7.5 cm (3 in) metal rings in the pan and spoon the potato mixture into the rings, pressing down well. Spoon a little of the cooking juices from the steaks over the potato pancakes and cook gently for 6–8 minutes, turning once, until crisp and golden.

Heat a little oil in a wok or large frying-pan and stir-fry the cabbage and garlic for 2 minutes until tender but still firm. Stir in the cream and a little seasoning and cook for a further 1–2 minutes.

To serve, arrange the pancakes on a plate and spoon over the stir-fried cabbage. Place the beef olives on top and garnish with the coriander sprigs.

To make good beef olives, the steak must be batted out as thinly as possible, so make sure you cut off any gristle or fat from the meat to make it easier to flatten out evenly.

**BRIAN TURNER**

# Creamy Beef with Crisp Oyster Mushrooms

This is quite similar to a classic stroganoff but with the crispy oyster mushrooms bringing it into the nineties.

 Onion, long-grain rice, rump steak, tomato chutney, oyster mushrooms, fine green beans.

Melt the butter in a large pan and cook the onion for 2–3 minutes until beginning to soften. Stir in the rice and cook for 1 minute, then pour in the chicken stock and half the wine. Bring to the boil and cook for 10–12 minutes until the rice is tender.

Heat 2 tablespoons of vegetable oil in a frying-pan and stir-fry the meat for 2–4 minutes; remove with a slotted spoon. Add 2 tablespoons of chutney, the lemon juice, cream and remaining wine to the pan and bring gently to the boil; season to taste. Stir in the meat strips and keep warm.

Dip the mushrooms into the milk and then the flour; deep-fry in hot oil for 2–3 minutes until golden brown; drain on kitchen paper.

Cook the beans in a large pan of boiling salted water for 3–4 minutes until tender but still firm; drain well. Gently heat the remaining chutney in a small pan.

To serve, pile the rice on a large plate, spoon over the beef and top with the warm chutney. Arrange the beans and crispy mushrooms round the edge of the plate. Sprinkle over the chopped parsley and serve immediately.

Oyster mushrooms or *pleurottes* are not the most flavoursome of modern 'wild' mushrooms but they can always be pepped up with garlic, herbs and spices.

## SERVES 2

50 g (2 oz) butter
1 onion, finely chopped
100 g (4 oz) long-grain rice
500 ml (17 fl oz) hot chicken stock
4 tablespoons white wine
Vegetable oil, for deep-frying
200 g (7 oz) rump steak, sliced into 1cm (½ in) wide strips
4 tablespoons tomato chutney
Juice of ½ lemon
200 ml (7 fl oz) double cream
150 g (5 oz) oyster mushrooms, halved if large
150 ml (5 fl oz) milk
6 tablespoons plain flour
200 g (7 oz) fine green beans
Salt and freshly ground black pepper
2 tablespoons chopped fresh parsley, to garnish

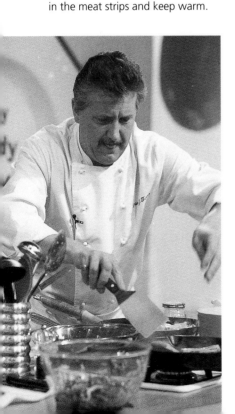

Creamy Beef with Crisp Oyster Mushrooms (page 129)

**Cranberry Lamb with Green Beans (page 132)**

# Cranberry Lamb with Green Beans

Chump chops, red onion, ready-to-eat dried apricots, dried cranberries, sultanas, runner beans, brandy.

Chump chops are one of my favouite cuts of lamb – they're good and meaty, and taste delicious with the cranberry compote.

**SERVES 2**

2 x 100 g (4 oz) boneless chump chops
1–2 tablespoons olive oil
1 tablespoon soy sauce
1 teaspoon clear honey
½ red onion, finely chopped
50 g (2 oz) ready-to-eat dried apricots, roughly chopped
25 g (1 oz) dried cranberries
25 g (1 oz) small sultanas
350 ml (12 fl oz) white wine
300 g (10 oz) runner beans cut into 1 cm (½ in) lengths
100 g (4 oz) butter
300 ml (10 fl oz) water
1 lamb stock cube
4–5 tablespoons brandy
2 tablespoons chopped fresh mint
Salt and freshly ground black pepper

Trim any excess fat off the lamb and tie into rounds with string. Brush with a little of the oil and season lightly. Cook in a hot griddle pan or heavy-based frying-pan for 1 minute on each side until well browned. Stir together the soy sauce and honey and pour over the lamb, turning to coat in the mixture. Cook under a hot grill for 4–6 minutes until almost cooked through but still a little pink in the centre. Transfer to an ovenproof dish, cover and keep warm.

Meanwhile heat the remaining oil in a frying-pan and cook the red onion for 5 minutes until softened. Stir in the apricots, cranberries, sultanas and 150 ml (5 fl oz) of the wine and cook for 15–20 minutes until the liquid has been absorbed by the fruit.

Cook the beans in a large pan of boiling salted water for 2–3 minutes; drain well. Heat 25 g (1 oz) of butter in a large, separate frying-pan and cook the beans for 2–3 minutes until tender but still firm; season with salt and pepper.

Place the remaining wine, the water and the stock cube in a pan and bring to the boil. Simmer rapidly for 5 minutes, then add the brandy and continue to cook until reduced by one-third. Whisk in the remaining butter and cook for a further 4–5 minutes to give a smooth, glossy sauce. Stir in the mint and season to taste.

To serve, pile the beans in the centre of a plate, place the lamb on top and spoon round the cranberry compote. Spoon over the brandy sauce and serve immediately.

Be careful not to over-sweeten the compote – it should have quite a tart flavour in order to complement the lamb.

NICK NAIRN

# Lamb Chops with Polenta and Garlic Mushrooms

This Italian-inspired dish offers a huge range of flavours and textures – it can be simplified by omitting the mushrooms. The lamb stock adds extra flavour to the polenta, but you can use chicken stock if you prefer.

Chestnut mushrooms, polenta, onion, tomatoes, lamb loin chops, French beans.

Pre-heat the oven to 220°C/450°F/Gas 7. Arrange the mushrooms, stalk-side down up in an ovenproof dish and drizzle over about ½ tablespoon of olive oil, the lemon juice and chopped garlic. Season well and bake for 5 minutes.

Meanwhile, place the lamb stock in a large pan and bring to the boil. Pour in the polenta in a steady stream, stirring constantly. Continue to cook and stir for 6–7 minutes until all the liquid has been absorbed and the grains are softened; season well, remove from the heat, cover and keep warm.

Turn over the mushrooms, drizzle with a little more oil and sprinkle over the parsley; return to the oven for a further 5 minutes until tender.

Heat 2 tablespoons of the oil in a frying-pan and cook the onion for 5 minutes until softened. Stir in the tomatoes, tomato purée and water. Simmer gently for 3–4 minutes then season to taste. Stir in the basil.

Meanwhile, cook the beans in large pan of boiling salted water for 2 minutes. Drain well.

Heat about ½ tablespoon of oil in a griddle pan or heavy-based frying-pan and cook the seasoned lamb for 3–4 minutes on each side until well browned but still a little pink in the centre. Remove from the pan and set aside to rest.

Toss the beans with about 1 tablespoon of olive oil and add to the griddle pan. Cook for 2–3 minutes until tender but still firm.

To serve, spoon the polenta on to a plate, place the lamb on top and scatter over the beans. Spoon round the sauce and arrange the mushrooms round the edge of the plate. Garnish with the chives.

I love green beans but am not a member of the current 'under-cook-your-vegetables movement'. I don't enjoy vegetables that are still very hard and crunchy; I like to cook my green beans for a full 4 minutes so that their flavour has chance to develop. And my very favourite way to cook beans is to dip them in a light beer batter and deep-fry them, although I have to admit, I did borrow that idea from Phil Vickery.

SERVES 2

150 g (5 oz) chestnut mushrooms
4–5 tablespoons olive oil
juice of 1 lemon
1 garlic clove, finely chopped
600 ml (1 pint) hot lamb stock
150 g (5 oz) polenta
1 tablespoon chopped fresh parsley
1 small onion, chopped
4 tomatoes, diced
1 tablespoon tomato purée
5 tablespoons water
1 tablespoon chopped fresh basil
100 g (4 oz) French beans
4 lamb loin chops
Salt and freshly ground black pepper
1 tablespoon snipped fresh chives, to garnish

# Curried Lamb Chappati Rolls

Onion, minced lamb, shredded coconut, tinned chopped tomatoes, tinned chickpeas, red pepper, okra.

I learned to make chappatis years before I became a chef so believe me, they must be easy. The self-raising flour makes the bread a little lighter but you can use all plain if you prefer.

## SERVES 4

100 g (4 oz) plain flour
2 tablespoons self-raising flour
1 teaspoon salt
4–6 tablespoons cold water
5 tablespoons olive oil
1 onion, finely chopped
2 garlic cloves, finely chopped
2 cardamom pods, cracked
1½ teaspoons ground cumin
1½ teaspoons ground ginger
1½ teaspoons cayenne
1½ teaspoons ground turmeric
1½ teaspoons garam masala
500 g (1 lb 2 oz minced lamb)
100 g (4 oz) shredded coconut
400 g tin of chopped tomatoes
400 g tin of chickpeas, drained and liquid reserved
1 tablespoon double cream
1 tablespoon chopped fresh basil
1 tablespoon chopped fresh coriander
1 red pepper, seeded and sliced
100 g (4 oz) okra, halved lengthways
Salt and freshly ground black pepper

To make the chappatis, place both flours and the salt in a large bowl and gradually add the water, a tablespoon at a time, to make a firm dough. Knead on a floured surface for 2–3 minutes until smooth. Quarter the dough and roll each piece out on a floured surface into a 15 cm (6 in) round. Heat a griddle or large, flat frying-pan and cook the chappatis for 2–3 minutes on each side until golden.

Heat 2 tablespoons of oil in a separate frying-pan and cook the onion for 5 minutes until softened. Add the garlic and cook for a further 1 minute. Stir in the cardamom pods and 1 teaspoon each of cumin, ginger, cayenne, turmeric and garam masala and cook for 1–2 minutes. Add the lamb, coconut, tomatoes and the liquid from the chickpeas. Stir well, then cook gently for 6–8 minutes until the lamb is cooked through. Stir in the cream, basil, coriander and salt and pepper to taste.

Meanwhile, place the chickpeas in a small pan with 2 tablespoons of the oil and the remaining cumin, ginger, cayenne, turmeric and garam masala and gently heat through.

In a separate frying-pan, heat the remaining oil and cook the pepper slices over a high heat for 2 minutes until beginning to brown; stir into the chickpea mixture. Add the okra to the same frying-pan and cook for 2–3 minutes until beginning to brown. Stir into the chickpea mixture and season to taste.

To serve, divide the lamb curry between the chappatis and roll up. Place on plates and spoon round the chickpea curry.

Get to know great convenience foods such as canned tomatoes and chickpeas used in this recipe. A few added spices and herbs can zip them up a treat!

**AINSLEY HARRIOTT**

# Tangy Lamb Kebabs with Satay Sauce

Lamb chump chops, onion, green pepper, beansprouts, spring onions, dried lemon grass, crunchy peanut butter, radishes.

Lamb is one of my favourite meats – perhaps it's that subtle sweetness that tickles my tastebuds and I'm sure yours will be too, once you taste this delicious dish.

### SERVES 2

2 x 150 g (5 oz) lamb chump chops, cubed
1 small onion, cut into 2.5 cm (1 in) pieces
½ green pepper, seeded and cut into
2.5 cm (1 in) pieces
Juice of 2 limes
3 tablespoons soy sauce
1 tablespoon chopped fresh coriander
2 tablespoons olive oil
200 g (7 oz) beansprouts
5 spring onions
1 garlic clove, crushed
1 teaspoon dried lemon grass

### FOR THE SATAY SAUCE

2 tablespoons crunchy peanut butter
120 ml (4 fl oz) white wine
3 tablespoons soy sauce
3 tablespoons olive oil
Pinch of lemon grass
Salt and freshly ground black pepper

Radish flowers, spring onion tassels and
fresh parsley sprigs, to garnish

Thread the lamb, onion and pepper on to four skewers and place in a shallow dish. Mix together the lime juice, soy sauce and coriander and pour over the kebabs, turning to coat them in the mixture.

Heat 1 tablespoon of olive oil in a heavy-based frying-pan and cook the kebabs for 1 minute on each side until well browned. Remove from the pan and cook under a pre-heated grill for 5 minutes, turning once, until tender but still a little pink in the centre.

Meanwhile, heat the remaining olive oil in a wok or large frying-pan and cook the beansprouts, spring onions, garlic and lemon grass for 2–3 minutes until tender but still firm.

To make the satay sauce, whisk together the peanut butter, wine, soy sauce, olive oil, lemon grass and salt and pepper to taste. Spoon into a serving bowl and garnish with a parsley sprig.

To serve, spoon the stir-fried beansprouts on to a plate and place the kebabs on top. Garnish with the radishes and spring onions and serve with the bowl of satay sauce.

If you are using bamboo skewers, make sure you soak them in hot water for a good half an hour to prevent them from burning during cooking.

**meat dishes**

136

# ANTONY WORRALL THOMPSON
# Sunday Best

This robust dish of lamb pies with vegetable rosti, dill carrots and mushroom gravy makes a meal to satisfy the heartiest of appetites – perfect for Sunday lunch.

 Ready-rolled puff pastry, lamb chump chops, potato, carrots, onion, button mushrooms, beer.

Pre-heat the oven to 220°C/425°F/Gas 7. Cut the pastry into four 10 cm (4 in) squares, place on a non-stick baking sheet and brush lightly with the beaten egg. Bake in the hot oven for 10 minutes until well risen and golden brown.

Meanwhile, make the vegetable rosti. Melt half the butter in a 20 cm (8 in) heavy-based frying-pan. Scatter in half the potato to cover the base of the pan, top with the carrot followed by a layer of the remaining potato. Season well and dot over the remaining butter. Cook for 15 minutes, turning once, until golden brown and cooked through.

To cook the carrots, place the water in a small pan, stir in the butter and sugar and heat, gently stirring until the butter melts and the sugar dissolves. Add the carrots and garlic and bring to the boil, then simmer rapidly for 5 minutes. Stir in the dill and cook for a further 2–3 minutes until the liquid evaporates and the carrots are tender; season to taste.

To make the gravy, melt the butter in separate pan and cook the onion for 5 minutes until softened and beginning to brown. Stir in the mushrooms and cook for 1 minute before adding the parsley, beer and stock. Bring to the boil and simmer for 5 minutes; season to taste.

Halve the lamb chops horizontally and flatten out with a meat mallet or rolling pan; season well. Heat the butter in a frying-pan and stir in the rosemary. Cook the lamb steaks for 5–6 minutes, turning once, until well browned but still a little pink in the centre.

To serve, halve the pastry squares horizontally and place a lamb steak in the base of each, pour over the beer sauce and replace the pastry lids. Garnish with the parsley sprigs and divide the pies between two plates. Cut the rosti into wedges and place on each plate with the dill carrots.

 Choose bitter, ale or stout for the gravy in this recipe – avoid using lager.

## SERVES 2

375 g pack of ready-rolled puff pastry
1 egg, beaten
2 x 150 g (5 oz) lamb chump chops
25 g (1 oz) butter
2 teaspoons chopped fresh rosemary

### FOR THE ROSTI
50 g (2 oz) butter
1 large potato, coarsely grated
1 carrot, coarsely grated

### FOR THE DILL CARROTS
300 ml (10 fl oz) water
25 g (1 oz) butter
50 g (2 oz) caster sugar
2 carrots, thickly sliced
2 garlic cloves, thinly sliced
1 tablespoon chopped fresh dill

### FOR THE MUSHROOM GRAVY
25 g (1 oz) butter
1 onion, thinly sliced
75 g (3 oz) button mushrooms, sliced
4 tablespoons chopped fresh parsley
200 ml (7 fl oz) beer
100 ml (4 fl oz) lamb stock

Salt and freshly ground black pepper
4 fresh flatleaf parsley sprigs, to garnish

ANTONY WORRALL THOMPSON'S

# Five Favourite Wines

**R**ules are made to be broken and wine rules are no exception. I can't understand people accepting without question the wine with food rules – have fun and play with food and wine combinations. Your rule should be, if you like the combination, go with it; your taste buds must be the final arbiter.Let's examine the rules and see how many we can break.

**Young before Old** The idea behind this is to build up to a crescendo during a dinner party with the masterpiece served at the end. However, the strong lingering tastes of fresh fruits and tannins of young wines can overpower

the subtlety and complexity of an older wine. Rather try the following: if drinking fruity wines, drink the older vintage first and the young later, but if drinking tannic wines such as red Bordeaux then the old rules apply. You can follow the progression from light to heavy, but not necessarily youth to antiquity.

**White before Red** This evolved because fish usually preceded meat, but in today's health-conscious world we may choose fish as a main course preceded by carpaccio of beef or a salad. So, you may choose a light Beaujolais for the carpaccio, and a Chardonnay for the fish.

**Dry before Sweet** In most cases this rule works, but there are exceptions. One that stands out is foie gras which you normally eat at the start of a meal with a sweet wine such as a Sauternes.

**White with Fish** It would be quite acceptable to stick to this rule without making many mistakes, as the acidity of white wine tends to cut through the fats and oils and the fishy taste, similar to squeezing a slice of lemon. But many of the New World Chardonnays tend to be oaked and very chunky, overpowering the flavour of the fish and lacking in acidity to cut through the fish oils. Nowadays too, many reds have a lighter style with very little tannin and wood, so are suitable for fish. As a rule, any young red will go with fish.

**Red with Red Meat** The new, rich whites of the New World, California, Australia and New Zealand can make great partners with a red meat stew or a spicy red meat dish. If the meat dish is rich you want a wine that can cut through this richness, something that is tannic and well structured.

**Five of My Favourite Wines**

*Tattinger Rose*: a light, elegant pink champagne perfect for any romance, and for caviar, oysters, lobster and the like.

*Petit Chablis:* not as meaty as a full-blown Chablis, but an elegant quaffing wine. A little green, but thoroughly refreshing, it goes with any fish, shellfish, chicken or veal.

*Chateau de Pibarnon:* a Provence Bandol Rouge, great with Mediterranean foods, a roast or a barbecue, the only Provence wine to drink.

*Sassicaia, Tenuta san Guido*: forget the classic red Bordeaux. If you can afford it this will blow your head off with its quality. Great with any meats, hearty casseroles, or to drink tucked up on the sofa with a lump of cheese.

*Joesph Phelps Late Harvest Johannesburg Riesling:* this wine will make you believe that some of the best wines on this earth are sweet. This Californian number is good with any non-chocolate pudding.

**ANTHONY TOBIN**

# Saucy Kidneys

Long-grain rice, lamb kidneys, red pepper, shallots, root ginger, sherry vinegar, spring onions.

Not always the most popular of ingredients, kidneys are often passed by in favour of liver and other offal, but in this dish, they are perfectly paired with rice and a tasty red wine and sherry vinegar sauce. Why not give it a go?

### SERVES 2

225 g ( 8 oz) long-grain rice
250 g ( 9 oz) lamb kidneys
4 tablespoons olive oil
Pinch of chilli powder
½ teaspoon ground ginger
1 red pepper, seeded and roughly chopped
3 shallots, finely chopped
2.5 cm (1 in) piece of root ginger, very thinly sliced
2 tablespoons sherry vinegar
2 tablespoons red wine
1 teaspoon soy sauce
1 teaspoon balsamic vinegar
1–2 teaspoons caster sugar
Salt and freshly ground black pepper

### TO GARNISH
1 tablespoon chopped fresh parsley
3 spring onions, finely chopped

Cook the rice in a large pan of boiling water for 12–15 minutes until tender; drain well.

Meanwhile, blanch the kidneys in large pan of boiling water for 30 seconds. Drain well, then cool under cold water. Halve horizontally then peel away the outer membrane and cut out the central core and any sinew. Place the kidneys in a bowl with 1 tablespoon of olive oil, the chilli powder, ground ginger and plenty of salt and pepper. Toss well together and set aside.

Place the red pepper in a food processor and blend until smooth. Stir into the cooked rice and season to taste; cover and keep warm.

Heat 2 tablespoons of the olive oil in a large frying-pan and gently cook the shallots and sliced ginger for 5 minutes until softened. Stir in the sherry vinegar and red wine, bring to the boil and simmer rapidly for 3–4 minutes. Add the soy sauce and balsamic vinegar and season to taste with sugar, salt and pepper; remove from the heat.

Heat the remaining olive oil in a separate, heavy-based frying-pan and cook the kidneys over a fairly high heat for 3–4 minutes on each side until well browned but still slightly pink in the centre. Pour over the shallot gravy and mix well.

To serve, pile the rice on to a plate and spoon over the kidneys. Garnish with the parsley and spring onions and serve with a crisp, green salad.

Don't be put off using kidneys – just take care not to overcook them and the meat will remain tender and succulent.

# Lambs' Liver with Stuffed Tomatoes and Potato Rosti

The combination of flavours and textures works really well in this recipe and the colours make it easy to present beautifully.

Potatoes, onion, baby white cabbage, caraway seeds, tomatoes, lambs' liver.

Place the stock, half the wine and the orange rind and juice in a pan. Bring to the boil and simmer rapidly until reduced by half.

To make the rosti, squeeze the grated potato in a clean tea towel to remove any excess liquid, then place in a bowl with the rosemary and plenty of seasoning; mix well together. Heat 2 tablespoons of the oil in a heavy-based frying-pan and sit two 10 cm (4 in) cooking rings in the pan. Spoon a quarter of the potato mixture into each ring, patting down well. Cook gently for 6–8 minutes, turning once, until crisp and golden. Repeat to make four rosti in total.

Brush a griddle pan or heavy-based frying-pan with the remaining oil. Add the quartered onion and cook for 8 minutes, turning occasionally, until golden brown.

Meanwhile, make the filling for the tomatoes. Heat the butter in a large frying-pan and cook the cabbage, garlic and caraway seeds for 2 minutes. Add the cream and the remaining wine and cook for a further 3 minutes until the cabbage is tender; season with salt and pepper.

Slice the top of each tomato and hollow out the centres with a teaspoon. Spoon the cabbage mixture into the tomatoes and replace the lids.

Dust the liver in a little of the cornflour and add to the onion pan. Cook for 1½ minutes on each side until well browned but still pink in the centre. Remove from the pan and allow to rest.

Dissolve the cornflour in a little water and whisk into the pan of stock. Bring to the boil, stirring continuously until smooth and thickened. Add salt and pepper to taste.

To serve, place the rosti on a large plate and place the liver on top. Arrange the stuffed tomatoes and the onions around the plate and pour over the sauce.

For rosti, avoid waxy or new potatoes. Choose floury potatoes such as King Edwards.

## SERVES 2

600 ml (1 pint) lamb stock
4 tablespoons white wine
Juice and grated rind of 1 orange
2 unpeeled potatoes, grated
2 teaspoons chopped fresh rosemary
3 tablespoons olive oil
1 onion, quartered
15 g (½ oz) butter
1 baby white cabbage, shredded
1 garlic clove, crushed
1 teaspoon caraway seeds
2 tablespoons double cream
4 tomatoes
350 g (12 oz) sliced lambs' liver
1 tablespoon cornflour
Salt and freshly ground black pepper

meat dishes

141

**PAUL RANKIN**

# Crusty Lamb Cakes with Mediterranean Vegetables

This is a great way to jazz up a wee bit of mince. Lamb works very well because of its slightly higher fat content but feel free to try it with beef, chicken or pork.

 Potato, onion, minced lamb, tomatoes, aubergine, courgette.

Spread the grated potato on a clean tea towel, sprinkle with salt and set aside for 5 minutes. Squeeze the excess water out of the potato by twisting the tea towel into a tight ball.

In a large bowl, mix together the chopped onion, minced lamb, basil, parsley, cumin and plenty of seasoning. Reserve a small walnut-sized piece of the mixture for the stock and shape the remainder into four even-sized cakes. Dip the cakes into the seasoned flour, then into the beaten egg and finally coat with the grated potato.

Heat the sunflower oil and butter in a large, heavy-based frying-pan. Gently cook the cakes for 8–10 minutes, turning once, until cooked through and golden brown.

Skin, seed and chop the tomatoes; set aside the flesh. Put the tomato skins and seeds in a pan with the reserved lamb mixture, garlic and stock. Bring to the boil and simmer gently for 5 minutes.

Brush the sliced vegetables with the olive oil and season with salt and pepper. Arrange on a baking sheet and cook under a hot grill for 6–8 minutes, turning once, until tender and golden.

Meanwhile, strain the stock into a clean pan and stir in the reserved chopped tomato, tomato purée, shredded basil and salt and pepper to taste. Whisk in the butter and cook gently, without boiling, for 2 minutes.

To serve, arrange the grilled vegetables on two serving plates. Pour over the tomato sauce and place the crusty lamb cakes on top.

Something I like to do is cook my meat a little ahead of time, then place it on a baking sheet. A few minutes before it's time to serve, I place the tray in an oven pre-heated to 200°C/400°F/Gas 6 until the meat is warmed through.

SERVES 2

225 g (8 oz) potato, grated
½ onion, finely chopped
350 g (12 oz) minced lamb
1 tablespoon chopped fresh basil
1 tablespoon chopped fresh parsley
1 teaspoon ground cumin
2 tablespoons seasoned plain flour
1 egg, beaten
1 tablespoon sunflower oil
15 g (½ oz) unsalted butter
2 tomatoes
1 garlic clove, crushed
300 ml (10 fl oz) lamb stock
1 teaspoon tomato purée
Small handful of fresh basil leaves, shredded
25 g (1 oz) unsalted butter
Salt and freshly ground black pepper

FOR THE VEGETABLES
2 tomatoes, sliced
1 small onion, sliced into rings
1 aubergine, thinly sliced
1 courgette, thinly sliced diagonally
2 tablespoons olive oil

# Grand Slam Lamb with Apricot Rice

Onion, long-grain rice, ready-to-eat dried apricots, runner beans, fresh tarragon, lamb leg steaks.

There's a lovely range of complimentary flavours here. The simply pan-griddled lamb enjoying the company of the apricot spiked rice and the thrilling tang of tarragon in the rich creamy runner beans. Well worth trying.

### SERVES 2

1 tablespoon sunflower oil
15 g (½ oz) butter
1 onion, chopped
100 g (4 oz) long-grain rice
300 ml (10 fl oz) chicken stock
50 g (2 oz) ready-to-eat dried apricots, finely chopped
150 g (5 oz) runner beans, cut into 2 cm (¾ in lengths)
5 tablespoons white wine
150 ml (5 fl oz) double cream
2 tablespoons chopped fresh tarragon
2 x 100 g (4 oz) boneless lamb leg steaks
1 tablespoon olive oil
Few drops of Tabasco sauce
Salt and freshly ground black pepper
Chopped fresh mint and flatleaf parsley sprigs, to garnish

Heat the sunflower oil and butter in a large pan and cook half the chopped onion for 2 minutes. Stir in the rice and cook for 1 minute. Add the stock, apricots and a little seasoning and cook for 10–12 minutes until the liquid has been absorbed and the rice is tender.

Meanwhile, cook the runner beans in a large pan of boiling salted water for 3 minutes until tender but still firm. Drain and cool under cold water.

Place the wine and remaining chopped onion in a separate pan, bring to the boil and simmer for 3 minutes. Stir in the cream and tarragon and continue to cook for another 3 minutes. Stir in the drained runner beans and cook for 2 minutes; season with salt and pepper to taste.

Brush the steaks with olive oil and season well. Cook in a hot griddle pan or heavy-based frying-pan for 4 minutes, turning once. Sprinkle over the Tabasco sauce and cook for a further 1–2 minutes until well browned but still a little pink in the centre.

To serve, spoon the apricot rice into two ramekins, pressing down well, then turn out on to serving plates and sprinkle over the chopped mint. Place the lamb steaks and creamy beans next to the rice and garnish with the parsley sprigs.

Tarragon is one of the great 'classic' herbs of French cooking and is widely used with fish, shellfish, chicken and vegetable dishes. It is also a vital ingredient in the famous sauce Béarnaise which is especially good with grilled meat. Tarragon vinegar can be easily made by putting a few sprigs into a bottle and then filling it up with white wine vinegar – it's ready to use after a couple of months and very nice in French dressing.

**PAUL RANKIN**

# Burn's Night Special

This recipe for fried haggis and potato rosti with whisky sauce is a good autumnal dish which is very tasty and satisfying. Try it with your own favourite sausage meat if you don't like haggis – I won't tell Nick Nairn!

Red-skinned potatoes, swede, curly kale, leek, haggis, Scotch whisky.

To make the rosti, spread the grated potato on a clean tea towel, sprinkle with salt and set aside for 5 minutes. Squeeze the excess water out of the potato by twisting the tea towel into a tight ball.

Heat 1 tablespoon of the oil and 25 g (1 oz) butter in a large frying-pan and scatter in half of the grated potato. Cook for 5 minutes one each side until golden brown. Repeat with remaining potato. Using a 10 cm (4 in) pastry cutter, stamp two discs out of each potato cake; keep warm.

Cook the swede in a large pan of boiling water for 2 minutes. Add the kale and cook for a further 2 minutes. Drain well and set aside.

Heat the remaining butter in a frying-pan and cook the leek, swede and half the kale for 5–6 minutes until tender and golden.

Meanwhile, heat the remaining olive oil in a separate frying-pan. Dust the haggis slices in seasoned flour and dip in the beaten egg. Cook for 3–4 minutes on each side until golden brown.

To make the whisky sauce, place the water in a small pan with the stock cube, whisky, Worcestershire sauce and tomato purée. Bring to the boil and simmer rapidly for 3–4 minutes until the sauce is thickened and glossy; season to taste.

Meanwhile, deep-fry the remaining curly kale for 2–3 minutes until crispy. Drain on kitchen paper and season with salt and white pepper.

To serve, place two potato rosti on plates and put a slice of haggis on top. Layer on another potato rosti and haggis slice then spoon the vegetables on top. Drizzle round the whisky sauce.

Haggis is a traditional Scottish sausage made with oatmeal, onion and various cuts of lamb offal. It is well seasoned, then packed into a sheep's stomach so it tends to look rather like a small football. Traditional haggis needs to be poached for several hours but nowadays you can buy a pre-cooked version which only requires re-heating. It is traditionally served on Burn's Night with mashed potatoes and turnips, otherwise known as 'tatties and neeps'.

## SERVES 2

2 red-skinned potatoes, unpeeled, grated
3 tablespoons olive oil
75 g (3 oz) butter
1 small swede, cut into 8 barrel-shapes or wedges
275 g (10 oz) curly kale, cut into 2.5 cm (1 in pieces)
1 leek, thickly sliced
1 x 454 g (1 lb) haggis, cut into 4 slices
3 tablespoons seasoned flour
1 egg, beaten
150 ml (5 fl oz) water
1 vegetable stock cube
1 tablespoon Scotch whisky
1 teaspoon Worcestershire sauce
1 tablespoon tomato purée
Vegetable oil, for deep-frying
Salt and freshly ground white pepper

# Glam Lamb Burgers and Ratatouille

Minced lamb, onion, red pepper, baby courgettes, pine nuts.

Minced lamb is now available in most supermarkets. It is very good value for money and often has more flavour than minced beef. Make up a double batch of these burgers and freeze some for another day.

### SERVES 4

50 g (2 oz) fresh white breadcrumbs
450 g (1 lb) minced lamb
1 onion, finely chopped
1 garlic clove, crushed
Grated rind of 1 lemon
1 tablespoon chopped fresh rosemary
1 egg, beaten
3 tablespoons olive oil
1 red pepper, seeded and cut into 1 cm (½ in) pieces
5 baby courgettes, diced
3 tablespoons white wine
75 g (3 oz) pine nuts
Salt and freshly ground black pepper

In a large bowl, mix together the breadcrumbs, minced lamb, half the chopped onion, the garlic, lemon rind, rosemary and plenty of salt and pepper. Stir in the beaten egg, then shape the mixture into four even-sized burgers.

Heat 2 tablespoons of olive oil in a frying-pan and cook the burgers for 5–6 minutes on each side until golden brown.

Meanwhile, heat the remaining oil in a pan and cook the reserved onion, the red pepper and courgettes for 5 minutes until softened. Stir in the wine, cover and cook for 3–4 minutes, then add salt and pepper to taste.

Heat a small non-stick pan and cook the pine nuts for 1–2 minutes, shaking the pan continuously, until golden brown.

To serve, spoon the ratatouille on to plates, place the burgers on top and sprinkle over the pine nuts. Serve immediately.

Nuts can be toasted successfully on a tray in a moderate oven, under a hot grill or in the microwave (follow the manufacturer's guidelines) but as they burn so easily, I prefer to 'toast' mine in a hot, dry, non-stick frying-pan where I can keep my eye on them.

**VALENTINA HARRIS**

# Perfect Prosciutto-stuffed Pork

Pork fillet, sliced prosciutto or Parma ham, tomatoes, courgette.

This is a delicious juicy meal with the flavour of the ham and pork balancing perfectly with the crisp, courgette salad.

### SERVES 2

350 g (12 oz) pork fillet, cubed

3 slices prosciutto or Parma ham, cut into strips

Grated rind and juice of ½ lemon

5 tablespoons olive oil

2 garlic cloves, crushed

5 tablespoons white wine

½ teaspoon red wine vinegar

3 tablespoons chopped fresh herbs, e.g. parsley, basil, coriander

4 tomatoes, roughly chopped

1 courgette, sliced into ribbons with a vegetable peeler

3 fresh basil leaves, roughly torn

Salt and freshly ground black pepper

Make a hole in the centre of each pork cube and stuff each with a strip of ham and a little grated lemon rind.

Heat 3 tablespoons of the olive oil in a large frying-pan and cook the pork cubes and any remaining Parma ham for 5–8 minutes, turning occasionally, until browned and almost cooked through. Add the garlic and cook for 1 minute, then pour in the wine and cook for a further 1–2 minutes until the pork is cooked through. Season with salt and pepper.

To make the vinaigrette, whisk together the remaining 2 tablespoons of olive oil, the lemon juice, vinegar and herbs. Add salt and pepper to taste.

Stir together the chopped tomatoes, courgette ribbons and vinaigrette. Transfer to a serving bowl and sprinkle over the torn basil leaves. Serve with the pork cubes.

Prosciutto crudo is mistakenly thought of universally as Parma ham. In fact, prosciutto comes from the Langhirano valley just outside the city of Parma. After being salted and trimmed, the ham is cured for about a year in specially ventilated warehouses, then it is trimmed and cleaned before being sold. Prosciutto crudo is expensive, but its price reflects the care and attention which has gone into making it. Delicious served in the classic way as a starter with juicy melon or ripe figs, it is also useful as an ingredient for all sorts of hot and cold dishes.

# Fruity Stuffed Pork with Pumpkin Sauce

A delicious autumn combination making use of two products – pork and pumpkin – that we would do well to use more often.

Onion, easy-cook white rice, sultanas, cooking apple, pork escalopes, Kabocha squash or other small pumpkin.

Pre-heat the oven to 220°C/425°F/Gas 7. Melt 25 g (1 oz) of the butter in a pan and cook half of the chopped onion for 3–4 minutes until softened. Stir in the rice and pour over the boiling water. Cover and simmer for 10–12 minutes until the grains are tender.

Meanwhile, melt 25 g (1 oz) of the butter in a large frying-pan and cook the remaining onion, the sultanas, apple, lemon rind, sage and garlic for 5 minutes until softened. Season well.

Beat out the pork escalopes with a meat mallet or rolling pin until very thin. Spoon the sultana mixture on top of each escalope and roll up tightly; secure with cocktail sticks. Heat the remaining butter in a skillet or ovenproof frying-pan and cook the pork rolls for 2–3 minutes, shaking the pan until well browned. Place in the oven and roast for 10 minutes until cooked through.

Bring a large pan of water to the boil and add the squash and stock cube. Simmer rapidly for 5–7 minutes until the squash is tender. Drain well and return to the pan. Purée with a hand-held blender, then stir in the cream and salt and pepper to taste.

To serve, spoon the rice on to a large plate and arrange the pork rolls on top. Spoon round the pumpkin sauce and garnish with the parsley sprigs.

For me, the best form of squash is the butternut. Pumpkins and squash are excellent cut into wedges and roasted with fresh thyme, whole garlic cloves and olive oil. Firm rind varieties should be stored at room temperature. Both squash and pumpkins are low in calories, fat and sodium and a good source of fibre, potassium and beta-carotene.

## SERVES 2

75 g (3 oz) butter
1 onion, chopped
250 g (9 oz) easy-cook white rice
600 ml (1 pint) boiling water
100 g (4 oz) sultanas
1 cooking apple, chopped
Grated rind of 1 lemon
1 tablespoon chopped fresh sage
1 garlic clove, finely chopped
4 x 75 g (3 oz) pork escalopes
1 Kabocha squash or other small pumpkin, skinned, seeded and cubed
1 vegetable stock cube
4 tablespoons double cream
Salt and freshly ground black pepper
Fresh flatleaf parsley sprigs, to garnish

**AINSLEY HARRIOTT**

# Roasted Rosemary Pork with Red Wine Sauce

For a rich, tasty, succulent meal, look no further than this – it captures the right blend of flavours, colours and textures and is made without too much fuss.

 Pork fillet, potatoes, pitted prunes, shallots, fine green beans, button mushrooms.

Pre-heat the oven to 220°C/425°F/Gas 7. Season the pork fillet then roll in the chopped rosemary until evenly coated. Heat the oil in a large frying-pan and quickly brown the pork. Transfer to a roasting tin and place in the oven for 20 minutes until cooked through and well browned.

Meanwhile, cook the potatoes in a large pan of boiling salted water for 10–12 minutes until tender.

To make the sauce, place the wine, prunes, shallots and stock cube in a small pan. Bring to the boil and simmer for 10 minutes until reduced by half.

Meanwhile, cook the green beans in a large pan of boiling salted water for 2–3 minutes until tender but still firm.

Melt 25 g (1 oz) of the butter in a pan, add the lemon rind and mushrooms and cook for 5 minutes until tender. Stir in the green beans and lemon juice and add salt and pepper to taste.

Drain the potatoes and mash well with the milk and remaining butter. Season to taste.

Stir the cream into the wine sauce and check the seasoning.

To serve, spoon the mash on to a plate. Slice the pork and lay on top of the mash. Spoon over the wine sauce and serve with the lemony vegetables.

 If you have a set of electric beaters, use them to mash your potatoes – they'll be the best you'll ever taste.

**SERVES 2**

350 g (12 oz) pork fillet
2 tablespoons chopped fresh rosemary
2 tablespoons sunflower oil
350 g (12 oz) potatoes, diced
150 ml (5 fl oz) red wine
50 g (2 oz) stoned prunes
3 shallots, chopped
1 chicken stock cube
100 g (4 oz) fine green beans, halved widthways
40 g (1½ oz) butter
Grated rind and juice of 1 lemon
100 g (4 oz) button mushrooms, quartered
3 tablespoons milk
2 tablespoons double cream
Salt and freshly ground black pepper

meat dishes

151

# Granddad's Criss-cross Pork

Long-grain rice, pork loin steaks, red onion, aubergine, fresh young leaf spinach.

Boneless pork loin steaks are a lean and tasty cut of meat and they're pretty economical too – but be sure to cook them all the way through. Here they are served with turmeric rice, aubergine slices and spinach. *Illustrated on page 2.*

## SERVES 2

120 g (4½ oz) long-grain rice
1 teaspoon ground turmeric
3 tablespoons olive oil, plus extra for brushing
1 tablespoon balsamic vinegar
1 teaspoon soy sauce
2 boneless pork loin steaks, halved lengthways
1 red onion, finely chopped
2 garlic cloves, crushed
1 teaspoon tomato purée
100 ml (3½ fl oz) white wine
1 tablespoon chopped fresh parsley
1 tablespoon chopped fresh basil
1 aubergine
250 g (9 oz) fresh young leaf spinach
Salt and freshly ground black pepper
Lemon wedges, to garnish

Stir the rice and turmeric into a large pan of boiling water and cook for 10–12 minutes until tender.

In a shallow bowl, stir together 2 tablespoons of olive oil, the balsamic vinegar and soy sauce. Season the pork, then add to the marinade, turning to coat in the mixture; set aside.

Heat the remaining 1 tablespoon of olive oil in a pan and cook the onion and half the garlic for 5 minutes until softened. Stir in the tomato purée, wine, parsley and basil and a little pepper; remove from the heat and cover to keep warm.

Cut the aubergine lengthways into four slices. Brush both sides of the slices with olive oil and season well with salt and pepper. Cook in a hot griddle pan or heavy-based frying-pan for 3–4 minutes on each side until tender and browned. Remove from the pan and keep warm. Cook the pork steaks in the same pan for 4-5 minutes on each side until cooked through.

Place the spinach in a large pan with the remaining garlic and a pinch of salt. Cover with a tightly fitting lid and cook for 2–3 minutes until wilted; drain well.

To serve, pat the rice into two ramekins then turn out on to plates. Spoon the spinach and the red onion mixture round the rice. Arrange the pork and aubergine slices on a separate serving plate and garnish with lemon wedges.

Spinach contains so much water that it's not necessary to add more to it for cooking. Simply wash the leaves and then cram them into a large pan, cover tightly and steam until wilted. Drain the spinach and see how much water has been released. Spinach is very high in vitamin C which is water-soluble, so cooking it in the minimum amount of water also helps to retain the vitamins.

# NICK NAIRN

# Gourmet Sausage Supper

Gamey-type sausages, such as venison or wild boar, work very well with the sweetness of the wild rowan compote in this strapping dish. Sautéed potatoes and stir-fried cabbage are the perfect accompaniment.

Venison or wild boar sausages, new potatoes, red onion, red pepper, wild rowan jelly or redcurrant jelly, Savoy cabbage, juniper berries.

Pre-heat the oven to 200°C/400°F/Gas 6. Prick the sausages with a fork and place in a roasting tin. Drizzle over the sunflower oil and season with pepper. Roast for 15 minutes, turning occasionally, until well browned and cooked through.

Cook the potatoes in large pan of boiling salted water for 15 minutes until tender.

Meanwhile, place 300 ml (10 fl oz) of wine and the stock cube in small pan and simmer gently.

Melt 15 g (½ oz) of the butter in a pan and cook the red onion and pepper for 5 minutes until softened. Stir in the jelly, the remaining 3 tablespoons of wine, the vinegar, coriander and salt and pepper to taste. Simmer gently for 5 minutes.

Meanwhile, heat 1 tablespoon of olive oil and 15 g (½ oz) of butter in a large frying-pan and stir-fry the cabbage and garlic for 4 minutes. Stir in the crushed juniper berries and salt and pepper to taste. Remove from the heat and cover to keep warm.

Drain the potatoes and halve lengthways. Heat 1 tablespoon of olive oil and 15 g (½ oz) of butter in a separate, heavy-based frying-pan and cook the potatoes for 5 minutes, stirring occasionally, until golden brown. Stir in the snipped chives and season to taste.

Gradually whisk the remaining butter into the reduced red wine stock to give a smooth, glossy sauce. Check the seasoning.

To serve, spoon the stir-fried cabbage on to a plate and pile the roasted sausages on top. Arrange the potatoes round the edge and pour over the wine sauce. Serve with the wild rowan or redcurrant compote.

With so many specialist sausage shops around Britain and supermarket meat counters becoming ever more cosmopolitan, there's no excuse for settling for those dubious-looking skinny, pink varieties any more. Be adventurous and have a crack at some of the more interesting types such as the 'merguez', a spicy Algerian sausage made from mutton or goat, the Spanish 'chorizo' or even a good old traditional pork 'Cumberland'.

## SERVES 4

8 venison or wild boar sausages, about 450 g (1 lb)
1 tablespoon sunflower oil
450 g (1 lb) new potatoes
300 ml (10 fl oz) red wine, plus 3 tablespoons
½ lamb stock cube
90 g (3½ oz) butter
1 red onion, chopped
1 red pepper, seeded and diced
2 tablespoons wild rowan jelly or redcurrant jelly
1 tablespoon red wine vinegar
2 tablespoons chopped fresh coriander
2 tablespoons olive oil
1 small Savoy cabbage, shredded
1 garlic clove, crushed
10 juniper berries, crushed
2 tablespoons snipped fresh chives
Salt and freshly ground black pepper

# Five Favourite Sandwiches

If I was put on a desert island and allowed only one ingredient, there's no doubt it would have to be bread. So to choose my five favourite sandwiches, I've really had to use my loaf!

Bread has always been a great companion to other foods and sadly over the years 'the sandwich' has become a shadow of its former self. For me, a sandwich can be an entire meal, full of exciting and sometimes surprising ingredients. But before I give you my top five favourites, here are some golden rules for sandwich making.

1 There are many different types of bread – ring the changes with them! Naan, pitta, rye, pumpernickel, tacos, foccacia, tortillas, muffins, granary … I could go on for pages.

2 Don't always assume that bread should be buttered. There's no need if you have an exciting, succulent filling. However, if you can't resist tradition, butter or a drizzle of olive oil is best.

3 Don't overdress or under-fill your sandwich. Keep the flavours interesting but make sur they're not over-complicated.

4 Remember, sandwiches can be hot, warm or cold, served closed, open, stacked or stuffed.

5 Finally, sandwiches are for anytime, anyplace, anywhere. So next time you have friends for dinner or a famished family to feed, check out these recipes!

**Whole Chicken Sandwich** Smother a chicken in garlic butter and black pepper and roast in the oven. Prepare a crisp salad, lightly tossed in a little lemon juice and olive oil, and stir together some mayonnaise and grainy mustard. Take all the essential ingredients to the table, arm your guests with a large plate and a napkin, and make yourself the most delicious designer sandwich!

**Oriental Chip Buttie** To give this buttie an oriental theme, sauce it up with peanut sambal sauce which is now available from most supermarkets. Cook up some thick chips, then stuff some warm pitta bread with shredded iceberg lettuce, grated carrot and sliced spring onions. Fill to the brim with the hot chips and drizzle over the warm peanut sauce. Eat at once!

**Pain Bagna** This is simply a stuffed loaf of bread. Take a large baguette, or any designer loaf, and split in half. Generously brush the inside with good olive oil or your favourite French dressing. Rub with a peeled garlic clove and layer up some sun-dried tomatoes, grilled sweet peppers, feta cheese, stoned black olives and some slices of avocado. Season with plenty of black pepper and fresh lemon juice. Sandwich the loaf together and press well before wrapping tightly in clingfilm or foil. Store, weighted down in a cool place, for 1–2 hours. To serve, cut into thick slices which will be stuffed with layers of filling - perfect for a picnic.

**Open Cheese Toastie Topped with Buttered Apples and Smoky Bacon** Toast some doorsteps of country-style bread. Mix together mustard, a little runny honey, grated, mature Cheddar and a nip of white wine or beer, if you have any handy. Spread this mixture over the toasted bread and return to the grill until bubbling and golden. Meanwhile, fry some chopped smoky bacon and a sliced apple in some butter until cooked and golden. Spoon over the cheese toasties and serve at once with a crisp green salad.

**Spiced Salmon Sarnie** Forget dainty salmon and cucumber sandwiches, this spiced fish extravaganza requires beer, not tea as its partner! Take some mini coriander naan breads and warm them in the oven. Brush some small, skinless salmon steaks with lemon juice and sprinkle with hot paprika. Fry the fish steaks for 2–3 minutes on each side. Fill the naan breads with baby spinach leaves, top with the hot salmon steaks, spoon over some cucumber and yoghurt raita, and don't forget the mango chutney!

# Pot-Belly Pork

Belly pork, potatoes, onion, cooking apple, green pepper, red cabbage, star anise.

The spicy cabbage mixture is slightly sweet and sour and packs a real flavour punch – enough to make a robust partner for garlicky potatoes and marinated belly of pork.

### SERVES 2

2 teaspoons Worcestershire sauce
4 teaspoons soy sauce
2½ tablespoons clear honey
2 teaspoons tomato purée
Few drops of Tabasco sauce
1 teaspoon dried mixed herbs
1 tablespoon wholegrain mustard
1 fresh rosemary sprig

### FOR THE PORK
300 g (11 oz) belly pork, halved
1 tablespoon olive oil
2 tablespoons red wine

### FOR THE POTATOES
2 potatoes
2 tablespoons olive oil
1 garlic clove, chopped

### FOR THE CABBAGE
1 tablespoon olive oil
1 onion, cut into 2 cm (¾ in) chunks
1 cooking apple, cored and sliced
1 green pepper, seeded and sliced
1 red cabbage, shredded
1 teaspoon balsamic vinegar
100 ml (3 ½ fl oz) red wine
25 g (1 oz) butter
2 star anise
1 tablespoon chopped fresh chervil
1 teaspoon caster sugar
1 tablespoon Greek yoghurt

Salt and freshly ground black pepper
Fresh chervil sprigs, to garnish

Pre-heat the oven to 220°C/425°F/Gas 7. In a large bowl, mix together the Worcestershire sauce, soy sauce, honey, tomato purée, Tabasco sauce, dried herbs, mustard and rosemary. Add the pork pieces, turning to coat in the mixture, and set aside.

Halve the potatoes lengthways and, keeping one end intact, slice thinly. Cook in a large pan of boiling salted water for 3 minutes. Drain well then place in a roasting tin, brush with the olive oil and sprinkle over the garlic. Roast for 20 minutes until crisp and golden.

Meanwhile, make the cabbage. Heat the oil in a wok or deep frying-pan. Cook the onion for 3–4 minutes until beginning to soften. Add the apple and three-quarters of the pepper and cook for a further 5 minutes. Stir in the cabbage, vinegar, wine, butter, star anise, chervil and sugar. Season with salt and pepper and cook gently for 5 minutes.

To cook the pork, heat the oil in large frying-pan and add the pork with any remaining marinade and the reserved green pepper. Fry for 8 minutes until cooked through, then remove from the pan and allow to rest. Add the red wine to the hot pan, swirling it round to mix with the juices.

To serve, divide the cabbage between two plates and spoon the yoghurt on top. Set the pork pieces to one side of the cabbage and pour over the red wine sauce. Garnish with the chervil and serve with the roast potatoes.

Belly pork is a great, cheap cut of meat. It has lots of flavour and the proportion of fat to meat means that the flesh doesn't dry out during cooking. It's great for roasting and barbecuing and I like to use it for making home-made sausages and terrines.

**PAUL RANKIN**

# Sausagemeat Surprise

This recipe for stuffed sausage patties with mini Yorkshire puddings and onion gravy demonstrates just how tasty simple ingredients can be when cooked well.

Tinned mushy peas, tinned sweetcorn, sausage meat, onion, brown ale, brown sauce.

Pre-heat the oven to 200°C/400°F/Gas 6. Begin by making the stuffed patty. Mix together the peas, sweetcorn, egg, sage, parsley and plenty of salt and pepper. Halve the sausagemeat and shape into two 15 cm (6 in) round patties. Spoon the pea mixture into the centre of one patty and place the second patty on top. Press the edges together firmly to enclose the filling. Heat the oil in a skillet or ovenproof frying-pan and cook the patties for 2 minutes on each side until golden, then place in the oven for 15 minutes until cooked through.

Meanwhile, make the mini Yorkshire puddings. Sift the flour and salt into a bowl and gradually beat in the eggs and milk to make a smooth, thick batter. Stir in 1 tablespoon of oil and set the batter aside to rest for 5–10 minutes. Lightly oil a 12-hole mini-Yorkshire pudding tin and heat in the oven for 5 minutes. Divide the batter between the holes and bake for 7–8 minutes until well risen and golden brown.

Meanwhile, make the fried onions. Heat the oil in a frying-pan and cook the onion for 5 minutes until softened. Stir in the garlic and sage and cook for 1 minute. Season to taste.

To make the onion gravy, heat the oil in a separate frying-pan and gently cook the onion for 10 minutes until softened and

golden brown. Pour in the ale and bring to the boil. Stir in the soy sauce, brown sauce and vegetable stock cube and simmer rapidly for 5–6 minutes until the liquid has reduced down to give a thickened, shiny gravy; check the seasoning.

Deep-fry the egg in hot vegetable oil for 2 minutes until the egg white is crispy but the yolk is still soft. Remove with a slotted spoon and drain on kitchen paper. Cook the sage leaves and parsley sprigs for about 30 seconds until crisp, then drain on kitchen paper.

To serve, pour the gravy on to a plate and arrange the Yorkshire puddings around the edge; top each with a teaspoonful of the fried onions. Place the stuffed patty in the centre of the plate and top with the deep-fried egg. Garnish with the crispy herbs.

Deep-fried eggs are a wonderful thing – they're crisp on the outside and soft in the middle. If you want to perfect making them, I recommend using a wok or a deep non-stick frying-pan. Heat 10 cm (3 in) of vegetable oil until hot enough to brown a cube of bread in 30 seconds. Break a good fresh egg into a saucer and carefully slide into the hot oil. Cook in batches of no more than three. Have a slotted spoon and kitchen paper ready. They'll take about 2 minutes to cook, but the best way to test them is to lift one out with a slotted spoon and press gently to check that the yolk has set – good luck!

## SERVES 2

### FOR THE PATTY
50 g (2 oz) drained, tinned mushy peas
1 tablespoon tinned sweetcorn
1 egg
½ tablespoon chopped fresh sage
½ tablespoon chopped fresh parsley
450 g (1 lb) sausage meat
1 tablespoon vegetable oil

### FOR THE YORKSHIRE PUDDINGS
50 g (2 oz) plain flour
1 teaspoon salt
2 eggs, beaten
150 ml (5 fl oz) milk
1–2 tablespoons vegetable oil

### FOR THE FRIED ONIONS
1 tablespoon vegetable oil
1 onion, sliced
1 garlic clove, finely chopped
½ tablespoon chopped fresh sage

### FOR THE ONION GRAVY
1 tablespoon vegetable oil
1 onion, sliced
440 ml tin of brown ale
2 teaspoons soy sauce
1 tablespoon brown sauce
1 vegetable stock cube
Salt and freshly ground black pepper

### TO SERVE
1 egg
4 fresh sage leaves
2 fresh flatleaf parsley sprigs
Vegetable oil, for deep-frying

**meat dishes**

# DESSERTS

**PATRICK ANTHONY**

# Toffeed Fruit Baskets and Chocolate Sauce

Plain chocolate, pears, red apples, brandy snaps, flaked almonds.

Everyday apples and pears get the star treatment in this elegant but easy creation. The chocolate sauce is very user-friendly, and can be made in advance and gently re-heated.

### SERVES 2

75 g (3 oz) plain chocolate
85 ml (3 fl oz) warm water
3 tablespoons double cream
50 g (2 oz) butter

### FOR THE FRUIT BASKETS
Squeeze of lemon juice
2 small unpeeled pears, cored and chopped
2 small red unpeeled apples, cored and chopped
4 brandy snaps
15 g (½ oz) flaked almonds
50 g (2 oz) butter
40 g (1½ oz) caster sugar
1 teaspoon ground cinnamon
Fresh mint leaves, to decorate

Pre-heat the oven to 200°C/400°F/Gas 6. Squeeze a little lemon juice over the pears and apples to prevent them from discolouring.

Break the chocolate into a small pan with the warm water and heat gently, stirring occasionally, until the chocolate melts. Stir in the cream and cook for 1–2 minutes to warm through, then whisk in the butter to make a smooth, glossy sauce.

Lay a piece of baking parchment or greaseproof paper on a baking sheet. Place the brandy snaps on one side of the tray, spaced well apart and scatter the almonds on the other side. Bake for 1–2 minutes until the brandy snaps are flat and malleable. Open out with a spatula, then drape over upturned cups or ramekins and leave to harden. Return the almonds to the oven for a further 5 minutes until golden brown.

Place the butter, sugar and fruit in large heavy-based frying-pan and cook for 4 minutes, stirring frequently. Sitr in the cinnamon and cook for a few minutes until the fruits are golden brown.

To serve, flood two small plates with the chocolate sauce and place two brandy snap baskets in the centre of each plate. Spoon in the caramelized fruit and scatter over the toasted almonds. Decorate with mint leaves and serve immediately, or for an alternative serving suggestion, place a scoop of vanilla ice-cream or dollop of Greek yoghurt on top of the fruit before scattering over the almonds.

To make this dessert even speedier, check out the ready-made brandy snap baskets now available – they're a real time saver, just be careful not to buy the chocolate-dipped variety.

desserts

**BRIAN TURNER**

# Kiwi Charlottes and Citrus Custard

This dish is best if made one or two hours in advance and chilled in the fridge until ready to serve. *Illustrated on page 158.*

Kiwi fruit, sponge fingers, Mascarpone, ready-to-eat stoned prunes, almonds.

Pour half the cream into a small pan with the milk and vanilla pod and heat gently without boiling.

Place the granulated sugar and water in a separate pan and heat gently, stirring, until the sugar dissolves. Add the orange and lime needleshreds and simmer gently for 8 minutes.

Line four ramekins with clingfilm. Place a slice of kiwi fruit in the base of each dish. Put the honey and wine in a heatproof bowl and place over a pan of simmering water. Stir occasionally, until well blended. Cut the sponge fingers so they are the same depth as the ramekin dishes. Dip the fingers in the honey mixture, then line the inside of the ramekins.

Whip the remaining cream until it forms soft peaks. Reserve 4 tablespoons of the cream and fold the remainder with the Mascarpone and diced kiwi. Spoon into the sponge-lined ramekins and fold over the clingfilm to cover. Chill for 15 minutes or until ready to serve.

Place the egg yolks and 50 g (2 oz) of caster sugar in a large, heatproof bowl and place over a pan of simmering water. Whisk until pale and thickened, then strain in the hot milk mixture and whisk for 2–3 minutes until thickened. Remove the citrus needleshreds from the syrup and stir into the custard; keep warm.

Heat the butter and remaining caster sugar in a separate pan. Stir in the prunes and cook for 5 minutes, stirring occasionally, until the prunes are coated in the butter toffee mixture.

To serve, spoon the prunes on to a plate and turn out the charlottes. Spoon or pipe a swirl of the reserved whipped cream on top of each charlotte and pour round the citrus custard. Top with the toasted almonds.

When whisking the egg yolks over the heat, do not let the water boil and don't allow the bottom of the bowl to touch the water or the mixture will get too hot, causing the eggs to set.

## SERVES 4

300 ml (10 fl oz) double cream
150 ml (5 fl oz) milk
1 vanilla pod, halved lengthways
100 g (4 oz) granulated sugar
300 ml (10 fl oz) water
Rind of 1 orange, cut into needleshreds
Rind of 2 limes, cut into needleshreds
2 kiwi fruit, 1 sliced, 1 diced
225 g (8 oz) clear honey
4 tablespoons white wine
75 g (3 oz) sponge fingers
4 tablespoons Mascarpone
3 egg yolks
75 g (3 oz) caster sugar
25 g (1 oz) butter
75 g (3 oz) ready-to-eat stoned prunes
25 g (1 oz) toasted almonds, roughly chopped

# Flapjack Stacks with Angel Hair

Flapjacks and candy floss were two of my favourite childhood treats – I've brought them together here, along with caramelized apples and a fruity sauce, to make a simple but very effective dessert.

 Apples, porridge oats, Lindisfarne Mead, raisins, dried cranberries.

Pre-heat the oven to 220°C/425°F/Gas 7. Begin by making the flapjacks. Melt the butter in a pan and add the sugar, syrup and oats, stirring until the sugar dissolves. Place a 7.5 cm (3 in) ring mould on a lined baking sheet and spoon in 3 tablespoons of the mixture, pressing down well. Remove the ring and repeat to make three more rounds. Bake for 8 minutes until golden, then cool on a wire rack.

To make the fruity sauce, pour the mead into a separate pan and stir in the raisins, cranberries, citrus rind and juice and the olive oil. Heat gently for 3–4 minutes.

Meanwhile, melt the butter in a heavy-based frying-pan and stir in the apples and sugar. Cook for 7–8 minutes, stirring regularly, until the apples are tender and golden brown.

To make the angel hair, place the sugar and water in a pan and heat gently, stirring, until the sugar dissolves. Bring to the boil and simmer rapidly without stirring until the mixtures turns golden brown. Using a metal spoon, quickly drizzle the caramel over the back of a wooden spoon to form fine strands; leave to cool and harden.

To serve, place two flapjacks on separate plates and spoon on a dollop of the whipped cream, top this with the caramelized apples. Place the remaining flapjacks on top and spoon over another dollop of whipped cream, decorate with the angel hair and pour round the fruity sauce.

The flapjacks, fruity sauce and caramelized apples can be made well in advance but try and make the angel hair as close to serving time as possible as the sugar absorbs moisture in the air and becomes sticky and softened in a relatively short time.

SERVES 2

25 g (1 oz) butter
4 apples, roughly chopped
2 tablespoons caster sugar
150 ml (5 fl oz) double cream, whipped to soft peaks

FOR THE FLAPJACKS
75 g ( 3oz) butter
50 g (2 oz) light muscovado sugar
2 tablespoons golden syrup
175 g (6 oz) porridge oats

FOR THE FRUITY SAUCE
150 ml (5 fl oz) Lindisfarne Mead
50 g (2 oz) raisins
75 g (3 oz) dried cranberries
Grated rind and juice of 1 orange
Grated rind and juice of 1 lemon
Grated rind and juice of 1 lime
½ tablespoon olive oil

FOR THE ANGEL HAIR
150 g (5 oz) caster sugar
300 ml (10 fl oz) water

# Plum Tarts with Greek Yoghurt

Strawberry jam, sultanas, seedless black grapes, damson wine, plums, ground almonds.

When I made these on the show my partner was an astrology fan with a sweet tooth – she thought they were out of this world.

**SERVES 4**

175 g (6 oz) strawberry jam
50 g (2 oz) sultanas
100 g (4 oz) seedless black grapes, halved
4 tablespoons damson wine or red wine
Pinch of freshly ground black pepper
4 tablespoons Greek yoghurt
250 ml (8 fl oz) double cream, lightly whipped
25 g (1 oz) butter
6 plums, halved and stoned
Caster sugar, to taste
Icing sugar, for dusting

**FOR THE PASTRY**

25 g (1 oz) ground almonds
225 g (8 oz) plain flour
100 g (4 oz) unsalted butter, chilled and diced
Pinch of salt
1 egg, beaten

Pre-heat the oven to 200°C/400°F/Gas 6. Begin by making the pastry. Place the ground almonds, flour, butter and salt in a food processor and whizz until the mixture forms fine breadcrumbs. Add the egg and continue to blend until the mixture forms a firm dough, adding a little cold water if necessary. Chill the pastry for at least 10 minutes, preferably an hour.

Roll the pastry out on a floured surface until 5 mm (¼ in) thick and use to line four 10 cm (4 in) tartlet tins. Cover each pastry case with a piece of greaseproof paper filled with baking beans and bake for 10 minutes. Remove the paper and baking beans and bake for a further 5 minutes until the pastry is lightly browned. Remove from the oven and leave to cool on a wire rack.

Put the strawberry jam in a pan and heat gently, stirring occasionally until melted. Place the sultanas and grapes in a separate pan and heat gently for 1 minute, then add the wine and black pepper. Simmer for 3 minutes until slightly reduced, then use a slotted spoon to transfer them to a bowl, draining well. Leave to cool, then fold in the Greek yoghurt and 4 tablespoons of the whipped cream. Add the jam to the mixture in the pan and simmer until thickened, then remove from the heat and leave to cool.

Melt the butter in a separate pan and cook the plums for 5 minutes, turning occasionally until tender. Taste and add sugar to taste. Leave to cool.

Divide the fruity yoghurt mixture between the pastry cases and arrange three plum halves on top of each. Pipe over the remaining cream.

To serve, place each tartlet on a serving plate and spoon round the jam compote. Dust with icing sugar.

A commercially made fresh, sweet shortcrust pastry is now available from supermarkets so if you don't have time to make your own, it makes a good substitute.

# Speedy Summer Pudding

I actually made four desserts in this programme but my simple summer pudding proved to be an extra-big hit.

 Frozen summer fruits, single cream.

Place the sugar and water in a small pan and heat gently, stirring until the sugar has dissolved. Bring to the boil and simmer rapidly for 2 minutes.

Place half of the summer fruits in a food processor with the icing sugar and syrup and whizz to form a purée.

Line a buttered 1.2 litre (2 pint) pudding basin with the bread, setting aside a slice for the top. Spoon in the whole fruit and place

the slice of bread on top, pressing down to seal. Pour over the fruit syrup then place a small plate on top. Place the pudding in the fridge and leave to cool completely.

To serve, invert the pudding on to a plate, slice into wedges and serve with cream.

 Make this dessert in the summer time and take your pick from the soft fruits around, but be sure to include both raspberries and strawberries.

## SERVES 4

50 g (2 oz) sugar
100 ml (3½ fl oz) water
500 g (1 lb 2 oz) frozen summer fruits, thawed
2 tablespoons icing sugar
12 slices white bread, crusts removed
150 ml (5 fl oz) single cream, to serve

desserts

# Fancy Fruit Cobbler

Pears, cooking apples, apricot halves in natural juice, candied stem ginger.

Fruit cobbler is a real heart-warming pudding and are super served with yogurt, ice-cream or best of all, lots of custard.

**SERVES 6**

225 g (8 oz) plain flour
1 tablespoon baking powder
Pinch of salt
50 g (2 oz) caster sugar
75 g (3 oz) butter, chilled and diced
Grated rind of ½ orange
6–8 tablespoons milk
1 tablespoon demerara sugar

**FOR THE FILLING**

50 g (2 oz) butter
3 pears, peeled, cored and chopped
350 g (12 oz) cooking apples, peeled, cored and chopped
2 tablespoons demerara sugar
2 fresh rosemary sprigs
Juice of ½ orange
400 g tin of apricot halves in natural juice
25 g (1 oz) candied stem ginger, chopped
Juice of ½ lemon
Icing sugar, to dust
Greek yoghurt, to serve

Pre-heat the oven to 220°C/425°F/Gas 7. To make the cobbler topping: sift the flour, baking powder and salt into a food processor. Add the caster sugar and butter and whizz until the mixture resembles breadcrumbs. Add the orange rind then, with the motor running, gradually add enough milk to form a soft dough.

On a lightly floured surface, gently knead the dough until smooth then roll out to a thickness of 2 cm (¾ in) and stamp out 8–10 rounds with a 7.5 cm (3 in) pastry cutter. Transfer to a baking sheet and brush with a little of the milk. Sprinkle over the demerara sugar and bake for 10 minutes until well risen and golden brown.

Meanwhile, melt the butter in a large frying-pan. Add the pears, apples, sugar, rosemary and orange juice and cook for 2 minutes. Add the juice from the tin of apricots and the ginger and simmer for 5 minutes. Add the apricot halves and lemon juice and simmer for 2–3 minutes until piping hot.

To serve, spoon the hot fruit into a serving dish and arrange the cobbler topping around the edge of the fruit. Dust with icing sugar and serve with the Greek yoghurt.

As an alternative way of presenting this dessert, place the fruit in six individual bowls and spoon a dollop of Greek yoghurt on top. Serve each portion with a 10 cm (4 in) cobbler.

**ANTONY WORRALL THOMPSON**

# Sexy Toffee Pudding

Light muscovado sugar, bananas, panettone.

This is one of my favourite **Ready Steady Cook** recipes and remains a regular feature on my menus.

**SERVES 2**

225 g (8 oz) butter
225 g (8 oz) light muscovado sugar
8 tablespoons golden syrup
5 ripe bananas
450 g (1 1lb) panettone, cut into 2 cm (¾ in) slices
200 ml (7 fl oz) double cream
150 ml (5 fl oz) milk

Pre-heat the oven to 230°C/450°F/Gas 8. Divide the butter, sugar and golden syrup equally between two pans, one of which should be large enough to hold 2 whole bananas. Heat gently, stirring until the sugar has dissolved. Bring to the boil and simmer gently for 3 minutes.

Meanwhile, peel the bananas and cut three of them into 1 cm (½ in) thick slices and add to one pan of toffee. Add the two remaining whole bananas to the other pan. Continue to simmer both, stirring occasionally, for 3–4 minutes.

Use half of the panettone slices to line the base of a 1.7 litre (3 pint) ovenproof dish, cutting them to fit. Place 150 ml (5 fl oz) of the cream along with the milk in a small pan and heat gently, without boiling, then pour half this mixture over the panettone. Spoon over the sliced bananas sauce and top with the remaining panettone. Pour over the remaining cream mixture and spoon over most of the toffee sauce from the second pan, reserving the whole bananas. Bake the pudding for 5 minutes until heated through and caramelized on top.

To serve, arrange the whole bananas on top of the panettone and spoon over any remaining sauce. Drizzle over the remaining 50 ml (2 fl oz) of cream and serve at once.

Panettone is a light Italian fruit bread, that is available attractively packaged from delicatessens and supermarkets. It can be substituted with brioche or any kind of light fruit bread.

KEVIN WOODFORD

# Fruity Clafouti and Banana-rama

This double dessert of classic French cherry clafouti with a banana mousse demands that you rest for at least three hours after consumption – very sturdy and not for the faint-hearted.

Tinned stoned black cherries in syrup, plain chocolate, marshmallows, coconut macaroons, Tia Maria, bananas.

Pre-heat the oven to 200°C/400°F/Gas 6. Lightly butter a 23 cm (9 in) pie dish and arrange a single layer of cherries in the base.

To make the clafouti batter, whisk together the flour, eggs, milk and sugar until smooth. Stir in the grated citrus rind and carefully pour the batter into the pie dish. Bake for 15–20 minutes until well risen and browned.

Meanwhile, make the banana mousse. Place the marshmallows in a small pan and heat very gently, stirring occasionally, until melted. Place the macaroons and Tia Maria in a food processor and whizz to form a crumb mixture. Mash together the bananas and lemon juice. In a separate bowl, whip the cream until it forms soft peaks, then stir in the mashed bananas and melted marshmallows. Spoon the crumb mixture into a buttered ring mould, pressing down well. Spoon the banana mixture on top, cover and chill for 15 minutes or until firm.

Meanwhile, break the chocolate into a heatproof bowl and place over a pan of simmering water. Allow to melt, stirring occasionally, until smooth.

Mix the cornflour with a little water to form a smooth paste. Place the cherry syrup in a small pan and stir in the cornflour mixture. Bring to the boil, stirring continuously, to make a smooth sauce.

To serve, turn out the banana surprise and decorate with the orange and lime slices. Remove the clafouti from the oven, dust with icing sugar and drizzle over the melted chocolate. Pour the cherry syrup round and serve immediately.

Clafouti can also be made with other soft fruit, such as raspberries or peaches.

## SERVES 4

### FOR THE CLAFOUTI
400 g tin of stoned black cherries in syrup
50 g (2 oz) self-raising flour
2 eggs
300 ml (10 fl oz) milk
50 g (2 oz) caster sugar
Grated rind of ½ lemon
Grated rind of ½ orange
100 g (4 oz) plain chocolate

### FOR THE BANANA SURPRISE
150 g (6 oz) marshmallows
6 coconut macaroons
2 tablespoons Tia Maria
2 bananas
Juice of ½ lemon
300 ml (10 fl oz) double cream

2 tablespoons cornflour
1 orange, segmented, and 1 lime, peeled and sliced, to decorate
Icing sugar, to dust

Fruity Clafouti and Banana-rama (page 169)

Orange Soufflé Omelette and Flaming Blueberries (page 172)

# Orange Soufflé Omelette and Flaming Blueberries

Dried blueberries, buttermilk, mineola oranges, fresh blueberries, whisky.

Dried fruits such as blueberries, cherries and cranberries are a fairly recent arrival in Britain. They have an incredibly intense flavour and I think they're fantastic! Here they add a much-needed lift to my soufflés.

### SERVES 2

50 g (2 oz) dried blueberries
100 ml (4 fl oz) boiling water
50 g (2 oz) unsalted butter
3 tablespoons plain flour
284 ml carton of buttermilk
6 eggs, separated
50 g (2 oz) caster sugar plus 1 tablespoon
Pinch of salt

### FOR THE ORANGES

2 mineola oranges, segmented
4 tablespoons caster sugar
1 tablespoon water
Juice and grated rind of 1 orange
Juice of ½ lemon
Grated rind of 1 lemon
100 g (4 oz) fresh blueberries
2 tablespoons whisky
Fresh mint sprigs, to garnish

Pre-heat the oven to 190°C/375°F/Gas 5. Place the blueberries in a bowl and pour over the boiling water. Leave to soak for 3–5 minutes.

Melt the butter in a pan, stir in the flour and cook for 1 minute. Remove from the heat and gradually beat in the buttermilk. Return to the heat and bring to the boil, stirring continuously, until smooth and thickened. Remove from the heat and allow to cool for 2–3 minutes. Stir in the egg yolks. Drain the blueberries and chop finely, then stir into the buttermilk sauce with the tablespoon of caster sugar.

In a large, clean bowl, whisk the egg whites with a pinch of salt until they form soft peaks then gradually add the 50 g (2 oz) caster sugar to make a stiff, shiny meringue. Gradually fold the meringue into the buttermilk sauce. Pour half the mixture into two skillets or ovenproof frying-pans and bake for 10–12 minutes until puffed and golden brown.

Meanwhile, make the flambéed fruit. Arrange the orange segments on a baking sheet and place in the oven for a few minutes to heat through.

Place the caster sugar and water in a small pan and heat gently, stirring until the sugar dissolves. Raise the heat and cook the mixture, without stirring, for 3–4 minutes until golden. Stir in the juice and grated rind of the orange and lemon and the fresh blueberries and heat through gently. Pour over the whisky and carefully ignite. Arrange the warm orange segments on a serving dish and pour over the blueberry sauce.

To serve, remove the soufflés from the oven and garnish with the mint sprig. Serve immediately with the flambéed blueberries.

If you're whisking egg whites, you need to ensure that the bowl and utensils are scrupulously clean. Any spots of grease or egg yolk will have a detrimental effect on the fluffiness of your meringue.

**KEVIN WOODFORD**

# Hot and Steamy Pudding with Raspberry Cream

If the microwave has a place in the kitchen, it's for this dish and any other 'steamed' puddings. It has the advantage of speed and the dish always retains a moist finish.

Mixed dried fruit, such as prunes, figs and apricots, tinned raspberries in apple juice, light muscovado sugar.

Soak the dried fruit in the fruit juice reserved from the tin of raspberries.

Beat together the butter and sugar until pale and fluffy. Gradually beat in the eggs, then fold in the flour. Drain the soaked fruit and stir into the sponge mixture with the milk.

Pour the golden syrup into a buttered 1.2 litre (2 pint) pudding basin. Spoon over the sponge mixture and cover with microwave film. Microwave for 4 minutes on PL9/High. Leave to stand for 5 minutes.

Meanwhile, make the raspberry cream sauce. In a large bowl, mash the raspberries with a fork. Stir in the cream, then whisk until the mixture forms soft peaks.

To serve, turn out the pudding and serve with swirls of the raspberry cream.

Do remember that a pudding cooked in the microwave will continue to cook after it's removed from the oven, so take it out while it is still slightly undercooked.

## SERVES 4

50 g (2 oz) mixed dried fruit, such as prunes, figs and apricots, chopped
300 g tin of raspberries in apple juice, strained and juice reserved
50 g (2 oz) butter, softened
100 g (4 oz) light muscovado sugar
2 eggs, beaten
100 g (4 oz) self-raising flour
2 tablespoons milk
2 tablespoons golden syrup
300 ml (10 fl oz) double cream

desserts

**VALENTINA HARRIS**

# Fruity Ooh-tiramis-ooh

Plums, Mascarpone, dark chocolate, sponge fingers, banana, clotted cream.

Tiramisu is a household Italian dessert that has many regional variations. It is quite rich and is purported to give lots of energy, hence its name that translates as 'pick me up'. This tiramisu does not use the classic coffee and chocolate combination as the ingredients in the shopping bag were slightly different; however, I think the resulting dessert is just as good as the original.

**SERVES 4**

5 plums
5 eggs, separated
250 g (9 oz) Mascarpone
4 tablespoons caster sugar
100 g (5 oz) dark chocolate
8 sponge fingers, about 50 g (2 oz)
1 banana, sliced
100 g (4 oz) clotted cream

Poach the plums in a small pan of boiling water for 5 minutes until tender. Drain well, remove the skin and stones then mash the flesh.

Beat together the egg yolks, Mascarpone and sugar.

In a separate bowl, whisk the egg whites until stiff, then fold into the Mascarpone mixture with a metal spoon.

Break the chocolate in half and, using a rolling pin, smash one half into small pieces. Stir into the Mascarpone mixture.

Grate the remaining chocolate and stir all but 1 tablespoonful into the clotted cream.

Dip the sponge fingers into the plum mixture to soften them, then divide between two tall glasses. Spoon over the poached plum mixture followed by half of the Mascarpone mixture. Top with the banana slices followed by the remaining Mascarpone mixture. Top with clotted cream and sprinkle with grated chocolate. Chill until ready to serve.

Mascarpone is an extremely rich and creamy cheese from Lombardy in northern Italy. It has a texture very like clotted cream and a mild, fairly bland flavour that makes it very useful in both sweet and savoury dishes. For a very simple dessert, serve it chilled with sliced ripe pears and a few walnuts.

**ROSS BURDEN**

# Raving Rhubarb Crumble with Citrus Curd

Rhubarb stems, oatmeal biscuits, fruit shortcake biscuits, fun-sized Mars bar, milk-chocolate raisin bar.

Rhubarb is my favourite fruit although it is really a vegetable. Its name comes from the Barbarians who brought it to Western Europe across the Rhu (the Volga). How very exotic for such a prosaic food! Here, I have combined it with citrus curd and chocolate sauce.

### SERVES 2

2 tablespoons caster sugar
250 ml (8 fl oz) water
1 vanilla pod
Grated rind of 1 orange
Grated rind and juice of 1 lemon
4 rhubarb stems, cut into 5 cm (2 in) lengths
2 tablespoons chopped fresh mint

### FOR THE CRUMBLE

2 oatmeal biscuits, crushed
6 fruit shortcake biscuits, crushed

### FOR THE LEMON CURD

Grated rind and juice of 2 lemons
Grated rind and juice of 2 oranges
50 g (2 oz) caster sugar
2 tablespoons cornflour
120 ml (4 fl oz) water
2 egg yolks
25 g (1 oz) unsalted butter
150 ml (5 fl oz) double cream

### FOR THE CHOCOLATE SAUCE

1 fun-sized Mars bar, roughly chopped
75 g (3 oz) milk chocolate raisin bar, roughly chopped
4 tablespoons double cream

### FOR THE CARAMEL

3 tablespoons caster sugar
1 tablespoon water
1 orange, segmented, to decorate

In a large pan, gently heat together the sugar and water, stirring until the sugar dissolves. Add the vanilla pod, grated citrus rind and rhubarb and simmer rapidly for 10 minutes until the rhubarb is tender. Strain the rhubarb, reserving the poaching liquid and discarding the vanilla pod. Transfer the rhubarb to a bowl and stir in the lemon juice and chopped mint.

Place the biscuit crumbs in a small bowl and pour over some of the poaching liquid; set aside to soften.

To make the lemon curd, mix together the citrus rind and juice and the caster sugar in a heatproof bowl. Dissolve the cornflour in the water and add to the bowl. Set the bowl over a pan of simmering water and cook for 3 minutes, stirring. Whisk in the egg yolks and continue to cook for 2–3 minutes, stirring continuously, until the mixture is thickened. Whisk in the butter, then remove from the heat and allow to cool. Stir in the double cream.

To make the chocolate sauce, place the chocolate in a heatproof bowl with the double cream. Set the bowl over the pan of simmering water and leave to melt, stirring occasionally until smooth.

To make the caramel, gently heat the caster sugar and water in a small pan, stirring until the sugar melts. Once the sugar has melted, cook without stirring until the mixture turns golden. Pour the caramel into the bowl of rhubarb along with 3–4 tablespoons of the poaching liquid.

Take a deep pudding dish and line the bottom with crushed biscuits. Pour over the lemon curd. Spoon the rhubarb mixture over the curd and drizzle with chocolate sauce. Decorate with orange segments and chill until ready to serve.

If the rhubarb stems are large and tough, they can still be used but must be peeled first.

## THANE PRINCE

# Snappy Ginger Biscuits

These home-made ginger biscuits knock spots off the shop-bought variety and they're incredibly simple to make. Store in an airtight container and eat within a couple of days (shouldn't be too difficult!).

 All ingredients from store cupboard!

Pre-heat the oven to 180°C/350°F/Gas 4. Place the butter, sugar, ginger and flour in a food processor and blend until the mixture forms coarse crumbs. With the motor running, slowly pour in enough orange juice to bind the mixture into a soft dough.

Place teaspoons of the mixture, well spaced, on a baking sheet and flatten each with a fork. Bake for 10–12 minutes until golden brown, then transfer to a wire rack to cool.

 Make the mixture ahead of time and store in the fridge for up to 24 hours. The cooked biscuits also freeze well.

### MAKES 20

100 g (4 oz) unsalted butter
100 g (4 oz) caster sugar
½ teaspoon ground ginger
175 g (6 oz) self-raising flour
Juice of ½ orange

## AINSLEY HARRIOTT
# Ainsley's Pancake Party

Ugli fruit, sultanas, bananas, Cox's apples, orange liqueur, such as Cointreau or Grand Marnier, single cream.

Many of us only make pancakes on Shrove Tuesday, yet they are so deliciously simple to make and can be filled or served with such a wide assortment of ingredients. Whether sweet or savoury, pancakes are just great and children always love them.

### SERVES 4

100 g (4 oz) granulated sugar
4 tablespoons water
1 ugli fruit, segmented

**FOR THE AMERICAN-STYLE PANCAKES**
225 g (8 oz) self-raising flour
250 ml (8 fl oz) milk
2 eggs, separated
1/4 teaspoon ground cinnamon
1/4 teaspoon ground mixed spice
Grated rind of 1 orange
200 g (7 oz) sultanas
Knob of butter

**FOR THE FLAMBEED FRUIT**
25 g (1 oz) butter
2 bananas, sliced
2 Cox's apples, peeled and sliced
Grated rind and juice of 1 lime
Juice of 1 orange
2 tablespoons orange liqueur, e.g.,
Cointreau or Grand Marnier
1 tablespoon icing sugar

**FOR THE FRENCH-STYLE PANCAKES**
100 g (4 oz) plain flour
1 tablespoon caster sugar
175 ml (6 fl oz) milk
2 eggs, beaten
1–2 tablespoons vegetable oil

150 ml (5 fl oz) single cream, to serve

Place the sugar and water in a small pan and heat gently, stirring until the sugar dissolves. Bring to the boil and boil rapidly, without stirring, for 3–5 minutes until the mixture turns golden. Add the ugli fruit segments to the caramel, turning to coat them in the mixture, then transfer to a tray lined with greaseproof paper and leave to set.

To make the American-style pancakes, beat together the flour, milk, egg yolks and spices in a large bowl. Stir in the orange rind and sultanas. In a separate bowl, whisk the egg whites until stiff, then using a metal spoon, carefully fold the egg whites into the flour mixture. Melt the butter in a heavy-based frying-pan and spoon in 2 tablespoons of the mixture, gently shaking the pan so it forms a 13 cm (5 in) pancake. Cook for 2–3 minutes on each side, then repeat to use up the remaining batter.

To flambé the fruit, heat the butter in a heavy-based frying-pan and when the butter begins to foam, add the sliced fruit and the lime rind. Cook for 1 minute, then add the orange and lime juice and cook over a high heat for a further 2–3 minutes until beginning to brown. Pour over the orange liqueur and carefully ignite. When the flames have died down, stir in the icing sugar.

To make the French-style pancakes, beat together the flour, sugar, milk and eggs to make a smooth batter. Heat a little of the oil in a pancake pan or small heavy-based frying-pan and add 2 tablespoons of batter to the pan, swirling it round to coat the base of the pan. Cook for 1–2 minutes on each side, then repeat to use up the remaining batter.

To serve, divide the flambéed fruit mixture between the French-style pancakes and fold over into quarters to enclose the filling. Stack the American-style pancakes four high, and arrange the caramel-ugli fruit on top. Pour over the cream and serve immediately.

The secret of a good pancake, especially the French-style crêpe, is based on a good thin batter which is used sparingly to make lacy pancakes. Once made, pancakes freeze very well.

# Peach Melba Meringues

Plain chocolate, whole brazil nuts, peaches, frozen raspberries, crème fraîche.

Meringues are really very simple to make and in this recipe they offer a nice change in texture to the peaches they are served with. I was given frozen raspberries but, of course, if fresh raspberries are in season use them.

**SERVES 2**

**FOR THE MERINGUES**
2 egg whites
100 g (4 oz) caster sugar
2 teaspoons ground cinnamon

**FOR THE CHOCOLATE NUTS**
50 g (2 oz) plain chocolate
75 g (3 oz) whole brazil nuts, toasted

**FOR THE POACHED PEACHES**
150 g (5 oz) caster sugar
3 tablespoons white wine
4 tablespoons water
Juice of 1 orange
4 cloves
2 peaches, halved and stoned
15 g (½ oz) butter

**FOR THE RASPBERRY SAUCE**
100 g (4 oz) frozen raspberries
1 tablespoon icing sugar
Fresh mint sprig, to decorate
100 g (4 oz) crème fraîche, to serve

Pre-heat the oven to 190°C/375°F/Gas 5. Whisk the egg whites until they form soft peaks, then gradually whisk in the caster sugar until the mixture is stiff and glossy. Fold in the cinnamon. Using two tablespoons, shape the mixture into nine quenelles (egg shapes). Place on a lined baking sheet and bake for 6–7 minutes until golden and set but still soft in the centre.

Break the chocolate into a heatproof bowl and place over a pan of simmering water for 3–4 minutes, stirring occasionally, until melted. Dip the nuts into the chocolate so that one half is covered. Leave to set on baking parchment. Using a greaseproof paper bag or a large fork, drizzle the remaining chocolate over the meringues.

To make the syrup for poaching the peaches, place the sugar, wine and water in a small pan and heat gently, stirring until the sugar dissolves. Stir in the orange juice and cloves; add the peach halves, flesh-side down, and simmer gently for 8–10 minutes until tender but still firm.

Meanwhile, place the frozen raspberries in a food processor with the icing sugar and blend to make a sauce.

To serve, flood two plates with the raspberry sauce and place two peach halves in the centre of each. Arrange the meringues and chocolate nuts around the edge and decorate with mint. Serve with the crème fraîche.

Chocolate melts very easily in a microwave. Break the chocolate into a microwave-proof bowl and cook on PL9/High for 1 minute. Leave to stand for 30 seconds, then stir with a spoon until melted.

**NICK NAIRN**

# Highland Fling

Now here's a couple of proper Scots dishes for ye to try.

 Scottish porridge oats, whisky, tinned Scottish raspberries.

## Cranachan

This is a very traditional dessert that is always made with oats, cream and whisky – but there are many ways to adapt this and make it your own – one of the best versions I've ever made contained fresh pineapple, Kirsch and toasted flaked almonds!

Dry-fry the oats in a non-stick pan for 4–5 minutes until golden. Transfer to plate and leave to cool.

Whip the cream until it forms soft peaks. Using a large metal spoon, fold in the whisky, honey, raspberries and cooled oats. Spoon into two glasses and chill until ready to serve. Decorate with mint leaves before serving.

## Hot Toddy

Oh what comfort a hot toddy offers to those in need of sleep on cold winter's night!

To make a hot toddy for one, place a double measure of whisky in a small, heatproof tumbler. Stir in the honey and the lemon juice. Top up with boiling water and drop in a couple of cloves. Serve immediately.

 Whisky is fantastic – it adds a unique, smoky flavour when used in cooking and is, of course, the traditional Scottish nip. If you are cooking with whisky, just use a simple blended whisky and save your best malts for drinking.

SERVES 2

FOR THE CRANACHAN
50 g (2 oz) Scottish porridge oats
150 ml (5 fl oz) double cream
2 tablespoons whisky
1 tablespoon clear honey
290 g tin of Scottish raspberries, drained
Fresh mint leaves, to decorate

FOR THE HOT TODDY
Double measure of whisky
1 tablespoon clear honey
Juice of ¼ of a lemon
Boiling water
2 whole cloves

# Six of the Best Gadgets

For well over ten years now, I've been enthusiastically investigating the almost bewildering array of kitchen tools and gadgets on offer to a seemingly insatiable public, who regularly remark on my gadget demonstrations for **Ready Steady Cook**. Fern calls me 'Inspector Gadget' and one viewer's letter even began *'Dear Gadget Guru'*!

The whole thing has become a kind of professional hobby and I'm constantly amazed by people's clever inventiveness, although it has to be said, not all the gadgets I've tested have been worth the time and trouble involved. Even so, I hope they never stop making them because life in the kitchen would surely be a lot less fun if they did!

Here, in no particular order, is my *'six of the best'* selection.

**Zester** This professional chefs' tool was the first 'gadget' I demonstrated on television and it provoked such a huge response from the viewers that it 'started' me off, so to speak. So what is a zester? It looks like a small, blunt vegetable knife, but five little holes are to be found in the downward curving end of the blade which you draw with firm and steady pressure along the orange, lemon or lime skin to produce pith-free strands of the 'zest'. Great for cakes, ice cream and puddings.

**Garlic Press** I have six different garlic-crushing gadgets including an electric model worth about £30! The very best of all of them is a new Swiss model (Susi by Zylis) which is very effective to use. Simply place the unpeeled clove in the compartment, then with the little piston-like pusher in position, squeeze the handles together. The finely crushed garlic comes out through the holes, leaving the entire skin behind for easy removal.

**Potato Ricer** There's always a big round of applause whenever I demonstrate this piece of equipment, which has clearly stood the test of time. In appearance, it's just like a giant garlic press with a hinged pusher attached to the upper handle which bears directly down on to the peeled boiled potato, forcing it through the holes on the other side from which it emerges like little, soft (fat-free), fluffy grains of rice. As well as potatoes, peeled and cooked parsnips, swede, carrots, apples and pears can be given the ricer treatment.

**Tomato Corer** About 15 years ago I acquired this from the USA and have treasured it ever since. Now available in the UK, this tiny tool neatly 'bites out' the hard, bitter, green core from the top of the whole tomato.

**Apple Corer** Another undoubted success, this clever corer and cutter works a treat. The stainless steel blades are set like the spokes of a wheel with the corer in the centre acting as the hub. One firm, downward movement neatly produces 12 cored segments. An indispensable kitchen gadget, especially when making the classic French apple pie *tarte tatin*.

**The Number One Tool** A good quality, well-sharpened knife is still, and always will be, the cook's most useful kitchen tool. Remember, you get what you pay for and a sound investment will reward you with years of good service. Most people only need two or three knives and my own favourite brands are 'Henckles Professional S range', 'Victorinox', who make the famous Swiss army knife, and 'Maxime Girard Sabatier'.

To sharpen, which you really should do every time you use your knives, I urge you to get the Chantry Knife Sharpener which requires no professional skill to use. It features crossed steels cleverly set on springs which rotate against the blade as it passes through the slot to give an excellent edge. To the serious cook, a knife is equal to the painter's brush and the violinist's bow.

**THANE PRINCE**

# Muffins with Zesty Crème Fraîche

Crème fraîche.

I really enjoy baking and muffins are so quick and easy to make yet they always pop out of the oven perfect every time!

### MAKES 12

225 g (8 oz) plain flour
2 eggs
2 teaspoons baking powder
100 g (4 oz) caster sugar
3–4 tablespoons milk
6 tablespoons vegetable oil
1 tablespoon demerara sugar

FOR THE ZESTY CREME FRAICHE
200 ml (7 fl oz) crème fraîche
Grated rind of 1 lemon
Grated rind of 1 lime
Grated rind of 1 orange
1 tablespoon Greek yoghurt
1 teaspoon caster sugar

Pre-heat the oven to 220°C/425°F/Gas 7. Place the flour, eggs, baking powder, caster sugar, milk and vegetable oil in a large bowl and beat well with a wooden spoon. Spoon the mixture into a non-stick, 12-hole muffin tin and sprinkle over the demerara sugar. Bake for 14 minutes until well risen and golden brown.

Meanwhile, make the zesty crème fraîche. Mix together the crème fraîche, citrus rind, orange juice, Greek yoghurt and caster sugar until well blended.

Serve the muffins warm or at room temperature with a generous dollop of crème fraîche.

Crème fraîche is a French-style thick, soured cream. It has a mild, tangy flavour that offers a lovely contrast to sweet desserts.

# Chocolate Roulade with Cherry Sauce

Chocolate and cherries are one of those classic combinations and with a good measure of double cream you're guaranteed a dessert to die for.

Kirsch, plain chocolate, tinned black cherries.

Pre-heat the oven to 200°C/400°F/Gas 6. Whisk together the eggs and sugar until pale and fluffy. Sift the flour and cocoa together then very carefully fold in to the eggs and sugar using a metal tablespoon. Pour the mixture into a lined Swiss roll tin and bake for 8–10 minutes until risen and just firm to the touch. Cool in the tin for a few minutes, then turn out on to a wire rack.

Whisk the cream until thick enough to form soft peaks, then stir in half the kirsch.

Spoon a tablespoon of the melted chocolate into a greaseproof paper piping bag and pipe swirls of chocolate on to a sheet of greaseproof paper. Place in the fridge to set.

Stir the remaining kirsch into the remaining melted chocolate with 2 tablespoons of the cherry juice. Pour into a jug and keep warm.

Spread the sponge with the whipped cream mixture. Spoon the cherries over the cream then roll up the sponge lengthways, peeling away the paper as you go. Transfer to a serving plate, decorate with the icing sugar, mint leaves and chocolate shapes and serve with the warm sauce.

Roulades can sometimes be a bit tricky to roll up. If you do have trouble, you can always halve the sponge and sandwich it together into a square cake – it will still look very impressive.

## SERVES 6–8

3 eggs
100 g (4 oz) caster sugar
50 g (2 oz) plain flour
25 g (1 oz) cocoa
300 ml (10 fl oz) double cream
4 tablespoons kirsch
100 g (4 oz) good quality plain chocolate, melted
425 g tin of stoned black cherries, drained and juice reserved
Fresh mint sprigs and icing sugar, to decorate

**Chocolate Roulade with Cherry Sauce (page 185)**

Fruity Fry-up and Citrus Sauce (page 188)

**PAUL RANKIN**

# Fruity Fry-up and Citrus Sauce

Pineapple, apples, pears, semolina.

This is a classic recipe that can made with almost any firm fruit. It's also a good base for many other desserts and can easily be jazzed up by the addition of freshly cooked crêpes or a few fancy biscuits.

### SERVES 4

1 pineapple
50 g (2 oz) butter
2 apples, peeled, cored and cut into 8 wedges
2 pears, peeled, cored and cut into 8 wedges
Juice of ½ lemon
4½ tablespoons caster sugar
250 ml (8 fl oz) white wine
5 egg yolks
Grated rind of 2 limes
Grated rind of 2 lemons
Juice of ½ lime
1 teaspoon semolina
Icing sugar and fresh mint sprigs, to decorate

Reserve a few pineapple leaves for decoration, then top and tail the pineapple and cut off the skin. Using the point of a small, sharp knife, cut out the woody eyes. Quarter the pineapple lengthways, then cut each quarter widthways into 1 cm (½ in) thick slices.

Divide the butter between two separate frying-pans and heat gently. When the butter is foaming, place the pineapple in one pan and the apples and pears in the other. Squeeze the lemon juice over the apple and pears. Add 1 tablespoon of sugar and 100 ml (4 fl oz) wine to each pan and cook gently for 5–6 minutes, turning the fruit occasionally, until tender.

To make the sauce, place the egg yolks in a heatproof bowl with the remaining sugar and wine and the lemon and lime rind. Set the bowl over a pan of simmering water and whisk until pale and thickened. Whisk in the lime juice.

Sprinkle ½ teaspoon of semolina into each pan of fruit, stirring until the juices have thickened.

To serve, spoon the fruit on to serving plates and spoon over the lemon and lime sauce. Dust with icing sugar and decorate with mint sprigs and the reserved pineapple leaves.

Here I've used a little semolina to thicken the fruit juices because I was unlucky enough to have it in my bag (it nearly gave me a heart attack!), but many other ingredients can also be used successfully to thicken sauces – the best are arrowroot, cornflour and potato flour which should be dissolved in a little cold liquid before being stirred into the sauce.

**PATRICK ANTHONY**

# Valentine Hearts

This recipe for Madeira-cake hearts with crunchy toffee almonds and vanilla chocolate sauce comes from a special Valentine's day programme, which proved to be quite a challenge but gave me a win. The almond topping is also sensational with ice-cream.

 Madeira cake, flaked almonds, plain chocolate, vanilla extract, strawberries.

Place half the sugar in a small pan with the water and slowly bring to the boil, stirring until the sugar dissolves. Boil rapidly, without stirring, until the mixture becomes syrupy but does not colour. Stir in the orange juice and remove from the heat.

Cut the Madeira cake in half lengthways and cut out four heart shapes. Place the shapes on a serving plate and brush liberally with orange syrup.

Place the butter, remaining sugar, milk and almonds in a heavy-based frying-pan and cook together for 4–5 minutes, stirring occasionally until golden. Spoon over the syrupy hearts.

While making the almond topping, at the stage where the almonds begin to brown, the mixture may start to separate. To correct this, add 2 tablespoons of cold water to the pan (taking care because the mixture will bubble up), then whisk vigorously to achieve a smooth, toffee sauce.

Meanwhile, break the chocolate into a small pan with the water, the vanilla extract and 3 tablespoons of the cream. Heat gently, stirring until the chocolate melts, then pour round the Madeira hearts.

Whip the remaining cream until it forms soft peaks and spoon little swirls on top of each heart. Decorate with the sliced fruit and mint leaves. Dust with icing sugar and serve immediately.

 The vital ingredient to look for on a chocolate bar label is the cocoa solids content and for cooking, 50% is the minimum recommended amount. Also widely available is the 70% chocolate which has an even more intense flavour although the 'experts' tell me that chocolate with cocoa solids content any higher than this is more unstable and quite tricky to work with.

SERVES 2

100 g (4 oz) caster sugar
100 ml (4 fl oz) water
Juice of 1 orange
1 x 200 g (7 oz) rectangular Madeira cake
50 g (2 oz) butter
2 tablespoons milk
50 g (2 oz) flaked almonds
100 g (4 oz) plain chocolate
3 tablespoons water
Few drops of vanilla extract
150 ml (5 fl oz) double cream
200 g (7 oz) strawberries, sliced
1 orange, cut into segments
Fresh mint leaves to decorate
Icing sugar, for dusting

# Snappy Syllabub and Lychees

Tinned lychees in syrup, stem ginger in syrup, grapefruit, sweet dessert wine, such as Muscat, meringue nest.

This spectacular dessert may seem a little fiddly but in fact only takes minutes to prepare – and everyone will be very impressed that you have made the ginger biscuits yourself.

### SERVES 2

400 g tin of lychees in syrup, drained
4 pieces stem ginger in syrup, drained and quartered

### FOR THE BISCUITS

100 g (4 oz ) golden syrup
75 g (3 oz) butter
1 egg
225 g (8 oz) self-raising flour
2 teaspoons ground ginger
Pinch of salt

### FOR THE SYLLABUB

150 ml (5 fl oz) double cream
2 teaspoon caster sugar
1 tablespoon grapefruit juice
3 tablespoons sweet dessert wine, such as Muscat
1 meringue nest, crumbled
2 pieces stem ginger in syrup, drained and finely chopped
½ pink grapefruit, cut into segments

Pre-heat the oven to 200°C/400°F/Gas 6. Stuff the lychees with the quarters of stem ginger and set aside.

To make the biscuits, place the golden syrup, butter and egg in a food processor and whizz until well blended. Add the flour, ground ginger and salt and blend again. Drop teaspoonfuls of the mixture, spaced well apart, on a non-stick baking sheet and cook for 5–6 minutes until golden brown.

Meanwhile, make the syllabub. Whip together the cream, sugar, grapefruit juice and 1 tablespoon of the wine until the mixture forms soft peaks. Stir the meringue and stem ginger into the whipped cream mixture.

To serve, place four or five stuffed lychees in two tall wine glasses, drizzle over the remaining wine then spoon over the cream mixture. Place the glasses on two serving plates and decorate the edges with stuffed lychees, grapefruit segments and ginger biscuits.

Tinned lychees are available from most supermarkets, but if you can't find any, substitute fresh or canned pineapple and simply add the extra ginger you would have used for the stuffing, to the cream mixture.

# Index

**A**

Anthony, Patrick 28, 41, *47*, 80, *80*, 99, 108, 121, 160, 182-3, 189
aubergine towers with bulgar wheat 26, *27*

**B**

beef
    Chinese-style noodles with a red wine glaze and aubergine fritters 125
    corned beef hash with sweetcorn fritters 124
    creamy, with crisp oyster mushrooms 129, *130*
    hot sandwich with tomato and avocado salsa 126, *127*
    mini wellingtons with Béarnaise sauce *118*, 120
    stuffed, with curried potato pancakes 128
    steak and pasta in a creamy mushroom sauce 121
black bream, fried with samphire and langoustines 58, 59
Britton, Fern 6, *6*
Burden, Ross 21, 38, 50-1, 54, 97, 113, *119*, 176

**C**

cassoulet with dumplings *19*, 20
Cawley, Richard 14-15, 43, 48, 56, *83*, 89, 106, 112, 116, 117, 190
cheese
    mozzarella bruschetta 40
    soufflé goats' cheese tartlets with crispy leeks and red pepper and walnut sauce *10*, 13
cheesy bake and split-pea cakes 25
cheesy broccoli soufflés with mushroom croûtes 37
cherry clafouti and banana mousse 169, *170*
chicken
    and prawn noodle stir-fry *90*, 91
    and watercress pasta 88
    fried with pineapple salsa 82, 89
    in crème fraîche sauce with broccoli and sautéed vegetables 105
    lemon, with fried thyme tatties 101
    livers with cabbage, mash and onion gravy 95, 96

paella with stuffed roasted peppers 100
parcels with Jerusalem artichoke sauce 84
    on a stick with saffron risotto 97
    ravioli with cream sauce 92
    spatchcocked poussin with parmesan patties 104
    spinach-stuffed legs with tumeric-braised potatoes and cumin onions 85
    vine leaf parcels with rice and tomato sauce 93, *94*
    with spicy sausage 98, 99
*chicken, five favourite ways* 86-7
chocolate roulade with cherry sauce 185, *186*
clams, with spaghetti 54, 55
cod
    and sweet potatoes 57
    fried steaks with potato cakes and green beans 78, 79
crab with coconut and spicy stir-fry 56
cranachan 181

**D**

*dinner parties, guide to successful* 102-3
duck
    glazed with couscous and onion rings 109
    with plums and pancakes 106, *107*

**E**

*East, flavours of the* 50-1

**F**

fish and chips 48
flapjack stacks with angel hair *162*, 163
fruit
    cobbler 166, *167*
    fry-up with citrus sauce *187*, 188
    pancakes 178, *179*
    pudding with raspberry cream 173
    tiramisu 174, *175*

**G**

*gadgets, six of the best* 182-3

ginger biscuits 177
gnocchi with spicy tomato sauce 16
Gregory, Mark 26, 52, *52*
guinea fowl with grape dressing 110, *111*

**H**

haddock
    exotic raspberry kedgeree 65
    pasta and baked tomatoes 72
    with potatoes, vegetables and cream sauce 69
Harriott, Ainsley 24, *24*, 37, 66, 68, 86-7, 93, 101, *101*, 128, 136, 141, 151, 178
Harris, Valentina 17, *17*, 148, 159, 174
hot toddy 181

**K**

kiwi charlottes and citrus custard *158*, 161

**L**

lamb
    chops with polenta and garlic mushrooms 133
    crusty cakes with Mediterranean vegetables *142*, 143
    curried chappati rolls 134, *135*
    kidneys with rice and red wine 140
    liver with stuffed tomatoes and potato rosti 141
    pies with vegetable rosti, dill carrots and mushroom gravy 137
    tangy kebabs with satay sauce 136
    with green beans and cranberry compote *131*, 132
lasagne with spinach and mushrooms 29
Little, Alastair 61, *61*, 69, 152, *152*
lobster in cream wine sauce with herb rice 60
lychees with syllabub and gingersnaps 190

**M**

mackerel, herby with sautéed sweet potatoes 66, *67*
Madeira-cake hearts with crunchy toffee almonds and vanilla chocolate sauce 189

Martin, James 78, 165, *165*
miso mullet with Japanese vegetables 81
muffins with zesty crème fraîche 184
mushrooms
  risotto 17, *18*
  stuffed with sautéed aubergines and cheese sauce 28
  with pasta, cream sauce and stir-fried vegetables 41
mussel duet 73, 74

**N**
Nairn, Nick 36, 55, 64, 70-1, 92, 96, 133, 153, 181, *181*
nutty tofu burgers and oriental stir-fry 21

**O**
orange soufflé omelette and flaming blueberries *171*, 172
ostrich steaks with potato galettes and stuffed mushrooms 113

**P**
pasta spirals with aubergine and tomato sauce 44
peach melba meringues 180
pheasant with bubble and squeak *114*, 115
plaice, fried with pea and mint mash 52
plum tarts with Greek yoghurt 164
polenta pick 'n' mix 32
pork
  fruity, stuffed with pumpkin sauce 149
  granddad's criss-cross 2, 152
  pot-belly, marinated with red cabbage and garlic potatoes 156
  prosciutto-stuffed with courgette salad 148
  roasted with rosemary and red wine sauce 150, 151
prawns
  hot and spicy with couscous 62, 63

Thai-style curry 80
*presentation, top five tips* 30-1
Prince, Thane 72, 125, *125*, 177, *177*, 184
pumpkin ravioli with sage butter 38, *39*

**Q**
quail, spatchcocked with couscous 112
quorn in puff pastry with Thai-spice vegetables 24

**R**
rabbit with mixed mash and caramelized prunes 116
Rankin, Paul 11, 23, 30-1, 45, 134, 143, 157, 172, 188
ratatouille pancakes 33
red mullet with Japanese-style vegetables 81
rhubarb and crunchy curds 176

**S**
salmon
  mille-feuilles with new potatoes and spiced courgettes 77
  seared with sweet potato and rocket and tomato salad 46, 53
  with courgette, broccoli and Hollandaise sauce 61
*salmon, five favourite ways* 70-1
*sandwiches, five favourite* 154-5
*sauces, five favourite* 122-3
sausage meat patties with mini Yorkshire puddings and onion gravy 157
sausages with wild rowan compote and stir-fried cabbage 153
skate with black butter and caper sauce, fennel rosti and warm salad 75, 76
speedy summer pudding 165
squid-ink risotto 49
stir-fry, Japanese-style with crispy tofu and nori rolls 22, 23

summer vegetable stack with chunky chutney 36
sweet-potato gnocchi with tilapia 68

**T**
*tables, tips for the best-dressed* 14-15
tilapia and sweet-potato gnocchi 68
Tobin, Anthony 13, 58, 88, 110, 140, *140*, 163
toffee pudding 168
toffeed fruit baskets and chocolate sauce 160
tofu
  burgers with oriental stir-fry 21
  crispy, with Japanese-style stir-fry and nori rolls *22*, 23
tortilla stacks with guacamole and refried beans 12
trout fillets with beetroot crisps 64
turkey burritos 108
Turner, Brian 12, 35, 57, 65, 77, 85, 115, 122-3, 129, *129*, 132, 161, 164

**V**
vegetables
  autumn pie *42*, 43
  oriental platter 45
venison with sautéed vegetables and Dijon mustard sauce 117
Vickery, Phil 25, 81, 104, 109, *109*, 124, 126

**W**
Waters, Lesley 29, 32, 76, 100, 154-5, 156, 166, 180, 185, *185*
*wines, five favourite* 138-9
Woodford, Kevin 16, 20, 33, 60, 102-3, 120, 169, 173, *173*
Worrall Thompson, Antony 40, *40*, 44, 49, 63, 73, 73, 84, 91, 105, 137, 138-9, 149, 168

**Y**
Yorkshire puddings with mixed vegetables, pepper and potato cakes and onion gravy *34*, 35